Flower Arrangement
from
Wild Plants

Violet Stevenson

Flower Arrangement from Wild Plants

with 8 pages of colour plates and 16 pages of monochrome plates

2227133
745.92

J M DENT & SONS LTD
LONDON

Made in Great Britain
at the
Aldine Press · Letchworth · Herts
for
J. M. DENT & SONS LTD
Aldine House · Bedford Street · London

ISBN 0 460 07844 5

contents

List of Illustrations, vi

illustrations

Photographs by Leslie Johns

colour plates

Between pages 88 *and* 89

List of Illustrations

one

Conservation and Cultivation

The title of this book is certain to cause consternation and perhaps even arouse fear in the hearts of some conservationists, so let me begin by saying that it is because I love our wild plants so much that I believe I should write about them. And I sincerely believe that anyone who may begin reading this book in doubt will finish it in agreement with me.

To many people, and especially those who live in towns and cities for most of the time, a bunch of wild branches, leaves and flowers is a memento of a pleasant walk along a lane, across a common, through a field or wood. For them picking wild flowers is both a pleasure and an adventure and it is an experience which, in my opinion, should not be denied them. The danger, so far as the plants are concerned, is that too often too many as well as the wrong species are gathered. And it is interesting (this is just one point which prompted this book) that lack of restraint is as bad for the flower arranger as it is for the conservationist. An arrangement of six bluebells is usually more effective and beautiful than one of sixty. One branch can speak of trees more explicitly than a pitcher full.

I think it is true to say that the wild flowers which have the greatest appeal to the largest number of people are those which grow in masses. Children love to be set down in a field white with daisies; you will see many cars drawn up near a field vivid with poppies; and how many times have you noted, perhaps with regret and even anger sometimes, how a bluebell wood draws pickers as a magnet draws nails, to mention only three samples.

The rarer flowers are usually less appealing to the public, and it often happens that those of us who are gardeners and care deeply enough take pleasure in finding room for these in our own plots. What we do not want, simply because we cannot properly control them, are those plants which are exuberant by nature. In the kind of garden my husband and I tend there is room for small drifts of cow parsley, even nettles and others, but they would be very unwelcome in most. Therefore these plants must remain wild. But more than that, they must be allowed to grow wild so that those who want to gather them should be able to do so. The danger of extermination comes from those authorities and others who use herbicides on a grand scale and not from those who want to gather a handful of wildings to take home.

Many of our roadsides are often flanked by ribbons of what are virtually lawns, and these have no right to be! They should instead be bordered by grasses (not grass) growing freely in ecological harmony with our native plants, weeds perhaps to some people but a constant source of joy to others.

Therefore I begin a book on arranging wild plant materials not with an exhortation to gather them where you will and enthusiastically but with a plea that all the dear, familiar, common flowers should be left and allowed to grow and increase. Nowhere in this book do I suggest that our rare flowers should be picked for flower arrangement or for any other reason. I recommend using only the most ordinary and prolific of plants, although I hope to suggest novel ways in which to display them. Wild rarities, in my opinion, are not for the flower arranger; they are for the nation, and I think that anyone who is fortunate enough to find them should enjoy them as they are, photograph them maybe, and then walk away and leave them growing to bring pleasure to someone else.

All this presupposes that everyone who loves flowers also knows which species can safely be gathered and which ought to be left, but this is not so. Perhaps this book will help those who have had little botanical experience to identify the 'safe' kinds. Certainly it will preach restraint. I have 'protected' some others by failing to mention them at all!

I am reminded of a wild flower arrangement competition I was once invited to judge. I thought fit to leave a polite note against one exhibit in which certain wild orchids were featured, suggesting that it was unwise to gather so many when, in fact, these were becoming too rare. Later I learned that the exhibitor grew them in her garden! I consoled myself for my well-meant error by hoping that others saw the note and took heed.

Many gardeners could help save and even increase our wild plants. After all, some of those we now regard as garden kinds once grew wild, the pretty columbine, for instance, and even some of the choicest of garden exotics are wild in other parts of the world. Those who have found certain acknowledged garden plants difficult to grow might have more success if they made room for those good-looking wild ones which grow naturally on their local soil.

Having seen Swiss lawns in spring, I often think we miss a lot by our insistence on having a weedless area of grass. Those little plots coloured like a cotton print, with daisies, speedwells, cuckoo flowers and others, must be the true essence of spring to the people who sit there and admire them with such obvious pleasure. And when the flowers have faded there is still a green carpet which can be kept mown and tidy.

Our garden is surrounded by well-cultivated farm fields, yet, even so, many a wild plant appears uninvited. Our maxim is, 'You can stay if you're pretty!' Consequently rose campion, speedwells, pink dead nettles and celandines (both of which in early spring colour and cover the ground as effectively as any bought bulbs), bell flower, soapwort, wood sanicle, woodruff, violets, cowslips, primroses, moon daisies and arums are a few which can be found there. Some, like the speedwell, have to be kept under control, but others are even encouraged to cover certain areas.

As gardening editor of *Woman's Realm,* as you would expect I receive many letters from readers, a surprising number of which seek information about growing wild plants. Some of them are both touching and haunting. Letters like the one from a reader in Coventry, who after I had written about cowslips on my page wrote to tell me that after reading my notes she had cried because she realized that she hadn't seen any since she was a girl. 'They used to grow all about here,' she wrote, 'and violets and primroses too, but they've all gone from the old places. I want to see them growing again before I die. Will they grow in my garden? Where can I get the seeds?'

Such a letter is typical of many, all asking about childhood flowers, and I often wonder about the many 'wild' and 'woodland' patches created in some semi-detached plot near an industrial town! It is so touching that people should want to grow them so much. One wonders why the seedsmen spend so much time and money on raising bigger and bigger, though often dwarfer and dwarfer, African marigolds for example, when so many people are crying out for the simple, tiny, undoubled flowers.

How happy I was to see a vanguard of cowslips appearing on the verges of the M5 this year—the same motorway at the sides of which hundreds of cultivated narcissi have been planted in a charming manner. These lift the heart. Perhaps someone responsible could find room for our native primulas alongside the daffodils and perhaps these could be followed by columbines, *Gladiolus illyricus*, meadow saffron and others which will do as well as the cultivated flowers and live in the grass.

So, once again, before I get on to gathering wild plants, here I am urging more conservation, this time with a plea to join in and grow a few of the most charming species, incidentally not necessarily good 'pickers', for yourself.

And not only flowering herbaceous kinds like the lilac-coloured *Cardamine pratensis* or cuckoo flower, a host plant, incidentally, for the delightful orange-tip butterfly which I am happy to say graces our garden, but shrubs and trees too. You will find few cultivars more beautiful than the wild hawthorn and few more appreciated by the birds, who in autumn feast on the berries; few trees more delightfully scented than the mountain ash, also a bird food reserve; no lovelier tree than a whitebeam whose leaves unfolding look like magnolias; no more enchanting berry than the spindle; no evergreen braver than the holly. And the wonderful thing is that all are on sale somewhere. There is no need for anyone to dig these up. They have been reared properly by nurserymen and so stand a splendid chance of growing to fine plants, which is often more than you can say for those pulled up from their environment and carried back in hot hands or thrown into the back of a stuffy car.

If you are either young or an optimist you can grow many of our native shrubs and trees from seeds or berries. A hawthorn raised this way will itself produce berries in less than ten years. So when you bring home a berried branch, pause before you throw it out because it is no longer fresh and decorative. It could be that it comes from a plant which is worth propagating. These 'seeds' could be sown and the plants passed on. I have more to say about this in my last chapter.

Not many people, even those who live all the time in the country, decorate their homes exclusively with wild plants. Quite often the wild materials are simply used as spinners-out of the week's flowers rather than as a substitute for them.

For instance, for various reasons many of the commercially grown blooms are sold with none of their own foliage, and so often these need supplementing if they are to fill and furnish a vase adequately. This is not easy to do if you have no garden.

There are few (indeed I can think of none) of the wild shrubs and trees that will not provide materials to go with either garden or bought flowers, although of course one tries to select companionable subjects. Furthermore wild plants offer the flower arranger a great range of 'natural' accessories and what I choose to call floradashery, as we shall see.

It is important to appreciate that the modern flower arranger sees all parts of a plant as a possible source for decorative materials, and for want of a better omnibus word all in this context are called 'flowers'. So we shall look not only for the actual blooms, but for leaves, seed stems, fruits of all kinds, stalks, roots, branches, skeletons and barks.

Where shall we find them?

Few places are more rewarding to the flower arranger than a patch of waste ground. Here one can often find many treasures. Poor soil, starved conditions, baking sun and dry roots sometimes result in the most glorious colouration in stems or foliage, so vivid indeed that even the humble dock or a trail of knotweed can assume distinction.

Starvation also sometimes produces Lilliputian versions of some familiar flower, which in its tiny proportions becomes almost jewel-like and precious. These mites are delightful for miniature arrangements of all kinds. Suitable ones can be pressed and used for plant pictures.

You are also likely to find many outsize leaves, some of them, like coltsfoot and petasites, reminders of spring flowers long since faded. Elsewhere dock, horse radish and dandelion seem to take on a new personality. The beautiful rose bay willowherb in autumn, the little convolvulus, grasses and seed pods, all may be gathered without harm to our countryside flora and used in home decoration.

Growing more lush, yet also in great variety, are hedgerow plants: from the turn of the year, when you are sure to appreciate the large individual leaves of ivy with good long stems which can be arranged at the foot of bought or forced daffodils, and the trails of smaller foliage which form the undergrowth and climbs warily up the mis-shapen hedgeplant trunks; through early spring which sees the wild arum unsheathe itself and jostle the fern-like foliage of the cow or hedge parsley; through midsummer with tendrilled vetches and grasses of all kinds reaching up through the hedge; to autumn when the brambles arch invitingly heavy with fruits and busy with insects, to winter again when the cow parsley and hogweed umbels, their seeds spent, glitter, frosted, skeletons in crystal against the empty morning sky, their fluted stems linked with diamante cobwebs.

Walk slowly along a hedgerow and you will journey through a compact, special world. The shrubs and trees which comprise the hedge may be very ancient, although they renew themselves each spring. They are likely to be an assortment, a multiracial community of blackthorn, blackberry, dogwood, willow, hawthorn, hazel, field sycamore, elm, holly, oak, privet, snowberry and others, depending upon the locality. Through them, running like a piece of embroidery, you will find the climbers, their species according to the soil and locality; black bryony, with its green flowers, followed by handsome though poisonous berries; honeysuckle; vetches in variety; wild roses and others, though you are unlikely to find the wild clematis on acid soils. And through the jungle of growth at the base of the hedgerow, more join the struggle to the light: greater stitchwort (which must surely have more nicknames than most other wild flowers), white, starry-flowered, so like the garden annual gypsophila to which it is closely related; the hedge mustards and dead nettles, some of which can be found with very long stems produced in their endeavour to reach up to the light. Such stems are sometimes too soft and lush for arrangement and they also need careful picking. Better, as a rule, are the plants which have come to terms with shade and grow more slowly, such as foxgloves, wild arums and ferns. And usually shade plants last longer when picked.

If the hedgerow grows atop of a sloping bank, this is likely to be studded with plants, but they will be those that have to hold tenaciously to their little bit of earth, and usually they will not be of great use to the arranger except for miniatures.

Damp, moist places, riversides, banks of streams and canals, the margins of lakes and ponds, swamps and the marshy lands themselves have their own ecological structure. There are a few trees, including my favourite alder, and many species of willow which often, surprisingly perhaps, are most decorative for the arranger when their stems are bare because of the glowing red, orange and tawny hues of their smooth barks, which glow in the winter landscape. These also have catkins in spring, not all of them the soft 'pussy' willows, but also others which are soft chick-yellow like those of the crack willow, which has fine, long, pendulous catkins among its new leaves.

There there are reeds, bulrushes, sedges, horsetails and the fine variety of grass-like rushes, most of which will dry and remain decorative the winter through. The burr-reeds, sparganium, have interesting shapes, meadowsweet is usually so prolific that one can gather the wiry stems of fragrant flowers without spoiling the display, and water plantain and arrowhead have leaves as handsome as any house plants.

Heaths and moorlands yield more than heather or ling, although this is the dominant plant as one would expect. It grows with many others, sometimes with the Scots pine, with gorse, bilberry, foxgloves, brooms and bracken and a host of mosses, lichens and fungi, many of which can be used by the flower arranger, although some are best for pressing or preservation and subsquent perpetuelle arrangement. (Perpetuelles is a name I created for dried or preserved plant materials and it appears to have been accepted into the English language.) The cup-like *Coltricia perennis*, for instance, found on heathlands on light soil, and especially where there has been fire, can be dried, mounted on false stems and used as a 'bloom'.

Broom and bracken are both very versatile and can be used both in their young stages and after drying or preservation.

Where you can see that there has been a heath fire at some time, explore the area for scorched roots and branches of gorse. These will be prickly no longer. Instead they are often beautifully twisted, gnarled, shaped and smoothed. They can play the same role in arrangements as driftwood, adding height, width, shape and even atmosphere (*see* Pl. 5).

On moorlands, which develop in acid, peaty soils, the ground is normally much wetter than on heathlands and often there are extensive areas of bog. Here the many species of the lush sphagnum mosses grow, although these are of more interest to the gardener than the flower arranger. However, there are likely to be drifts of the common cotton grass, *Eriophorum angustifolium*, not really a grass but a member of the sedge or cyperaceae family. It is worth gathering and either drying or pressing.

You are likely to find many lichens, some growing in dense cushions among the other plants. These can be used in Christmas decorations.

Meadows are the places to find dainty grasses, although of course you should not walk in them if they are to be cropped for hay. Often there will be plenty of grasses at the margins where the mowing machine is unlikely to reach. Here also are the sweet clover, tiny field daisy and the larger moon or ox-eye daisy, sorrel, yellow rattle and many others which will be described later.

Gardens too can produce wild plant materials, and there is many a weed discovered growing unchecked and undetected which is really far too handsome to throw on the compost heap and which can act as a 'stand-in' for choicer flowers.

Materials which can be used in dried or perpetuelle arrangements are to be found almost everywhere, even on a walk through a city park, where branches of 'buttons' from the London plane trees and fallen leaves of all kinds often litter the ground after a gale or a heavy shower. Seed stems are in a great variety of shape, form, texture and size, sufficient for every kind of perpetuelle decoration, whether these be in containers, mounted on plaques of various kinds, assembled in swags, ropes and garlands.

The area under trees is often a treasure store for the flower arranger. Here are to be found well-studded yet graceful branches of larch cones like wooden flowers, and under the Scots pine large individual cones for which there are a hundred uses; sometimes a branch or two of the tufted, deep green needles can be found as well; early jettisoned branches of autumnal-coloured oak leaves can be dried or preserved if they are still fresh; seed cases and fruits of all kinds, beech mast, acorns, conkers and sycamore keys, for example; skeleton and partly skeletonized leaves which can be bleached and finished off at home; fallen leaves of all kinds which can be ironed or pressed between sheets of newspaper under heavy weights.

One would expect a wood or forest to be productive of all kinds of plant materials, and so it is, although some woods are more fertile in this respect than others. Much depends on the dominant trees. In some woods, those on the highest ground, these are pine and birch. In these you can expect to find fungi not met with where beech and oak grow. On sandy soils you will often find 'dry' oak woods which, in hilly country, lodge different plants from those they hold lower down. On the hills you can expect to find gorse, ling and bracken, lower down there should be drifts of foxgloves. But where the soil is of a clay nature and the oakwood is 'damp', hazels flourish in the lightly dappled shade of the trees, and with the hazels come many herbaceous plants, including ferns.

Beech woods are to be found on chalk and lime soils. Where these are ancient and the trees spreading and dense, few plants can flourish beneath them, although the good leafmould is so fertile. Yet at the edges and in clearings the plants are delightful and quite varied, although you will not find foxgloves, for these like an acid soil, but you will find bluebells.

Like many other people I am saddened when I see great sheaves of bluebells borne homewards at the end of a hot day, already wilting and discolouring. It is a tribute to the plant's vigour and adaptability that there are still bluebell drifts and woods to touch our hearts with their beauty.

Some time before the war I was interested to read an account of experiments which proved that bluebells increased more where the flowers were pulled than they did either where they were plucked or where they were left to seed.

This may surprise the reader, but pulling the stems damages the base of the bulb in such a way that some division is caused. The Dutch use a similar method to increase stocks of cultivated hyacinths. However, what the experimenter discovered, which is of greater importance, is that it was the trampling on the foliage which tended eventually to kill the plants. So tread softly!

When you find bluebells, stay your hand a while and consider that most of the flowers' beauty lies in the sweet and touching way the stem arches as it bears its bell-shaped blooms. This is the way they should be arranged in the vase. Gather no more than are likely to be arranged in such a way as shows their loveliness to advantage, as few as you would buy if they were on sale. When you gather them pull the stems, but before you arrange them cut off the white portion that once was hidden from the sunlight.

Bluebell bulbs used to be a source of starch, and I have found that a little carbohydrate in the water keeps them fresh longer than if they are given plain water. You will find details of preparation on page 36.

Although I love the fresh flowers, my greatest use for bluebells comes later in the year when the woods are full of their pale ghosts, tall papery stems studded with cases ripe and rattling with black, shining seeds. Shake out these and use the seed stems for dried arrangements.

There are many mixed woods, like those near my home, which are filled with a fine variety of plants. Others are artificially planted by the Forestry Commission, and may not contain much under-growth, although there are many decorative materials to be found at their margins. And in damp places woods will be of alders and willows, supporting their own special flora.

You can walk through the woods, and by collecting no more than a handful of items find enough of great diversity to make an unusual and often long-lasting arrangement.

There are many bark plants, some so humble as to be no more than the green colouring on a bole, but there are also larger epiphytes, lichens, mosses, liverworts and one type of fern, poly-podium or polypody.

You can often find pieces of bark or log already prettily colonized by a variety of plants. If you take these home, stand them on a shallow vessel, a tray or a deep plate. This need not be conspicuous and should not dominate the natural material. You should keep the little 'wood' well sprayed with clean water so that the plants remain moist and green. The receptacle is really to collect surplus water and protect the furniture.

Each type of woodland has its own fungi, as I have already noted, although there are a few which are to be found more widely distributed and can be found in mixed woodlands. Some of these are parasitic on the living trees, while others grow on dead wood or perhaps cling to the stump of a fallen tree.

Many of these are the bracket fungi, so named because of the way they grow. I find these both attractive and useful and I employ them not only as part of the flower arrangement in a container but sometimes as the container itself. You will find them in conifer woods and in birch woods, where they are usually coloured in greys and silver which harmonize with the bark of the trees. Yet actually the colour of some of them is very variable, like that of the *Trametes versicolor*, which is one of my favourites, for I admire the velvety surfaces of the 'oysters'. Bracket fungi in oak woods are as magnificent as the trees which harbour them. There is the great dryad's saddle, also to be found growing on elm and other trees, the beefsteak fungus and the grifola, with bright yellow undersides. There are also others. Mixed woodlands hold a great assortment of all kinds of fungi, many of which can be dried and used again and again.

Whether or not you use fungi in your flower arrangements will depend to a great extent on your personal tastes as well as the style of arrangements you prefer to make. Most of them lend themselves best to picture story designs (*see* p. 25), although I have used them in large massed arrangements. They do not blend with every kind of material, as you can imagine (*see* Pls. 1, 3, 4, 6).

Much more versatile, and harmonizing as beautifully with choice bought blooms as with a bunch of wild berries, are the lichen-covered branches one can find in so many localities, but especially in those areas where there is a heavy content of moisture in the air. I remember with pleasure picnicking by a Scottish loch with conifers making a shade over us, their branches festooned with the lovely long fringes of grey-green lichen. A search over the ground later resulted in finding many beautiful windfalls.

Like most other plants, lichens vary considerably. Some are a soft jade grey, while there are others which are yellow. Not all grow on trees, but those that do are usually worth having.

two

Beachcomber's Treasure

For me the seaside is a place from which I always come away laden with a wealth of materials to be used later in all kinds of arrangements. Some of my most treasured floradashery is marine in origin. On the seashore itself there are the many and varied accessories which bring originality and individuality to all kinds of arrangements. I look for the large pieces of flat stone, thin enough to be used as a base either for an arrangement which is container-held, or perhaps for one which will be assembled on the stone itself. These ready-made slabs, soft in outline and the colour of the local rocks, are in a variety of soft, pleasing hues, rose-red, grey-blue, charcoal and sand colour. Some are marbled and patterned by the other rocks and minerals merged with them. All, because they are natural products, harmonize with flowers.

Although they appear to be comparatively smooth, these stone bases should not be set down on finely polished furniture, for they are bound to mark or scratch it. Fortunately it is a simple matter to give the stones a protective base by using green felt Fablon, a contact fabric which has one surface highly adhesive, the other felted.

Rusty brown flints and what prove on closer inspection to be bones, shaped like some miniature Henry Moore sculpture, are well worth collecting. Sometimes I use the heavy ones to hold down recalcitrant stems of weighty blossom, horse chestnut, for example, which in a vase often has to be arranged at a completely different angle from that in which it grew on the tree. Besides being fascinating to study, the sculptured shapes of the bones are also convenient and can be used to embrace and hold a stem at its base, to separate it from its neighbours.

Smooth pebbles, especially those which colour prettily under water, are useful for hiding pinholders (pieces of heavy metal from which arise a mass of pinpoints) and to strew on the floor of some large shallow container to add interest and colour. They look well in glass and can be used on occasions as a stemholder. In this case put the pebbles in gradually (and carefully!), propping the stem or stems at the required angle as you fill the glass.

Coloured shells of all kinds serve the same purpose and these are best sorted into their hues. For instance, I like to use yellow periwinkles with yellow flowers at those times of the year when blooms are scarce. And they look well with other flowers. Yellow suits most flowers, for if you consider it, most have some of this colour in their make-up. The hue of the shells supplements the floral colour, and the arrangement in which they are used is all the more interesting for their inclusion. Imagine, for instance, a few kingcups grouped at the side of a glass bowl, the floor of which is strewn with yellow shells, their colour deepened, their size magnified by the combination of clear water and the glass.

Blue mussel shells look well, as you would expect, with blue flowers or those colours which are analogous or complementary to blue. I also like to use these under water. Sometimes you can find a stone or a larger shell of some other species on which small blue mussels are thickly clustered. Imagine a few bluebells, a fern frond or two, a few fresh green arum leaves, or perhaps instead the whorled stems of starry-tipped woodruff, rising from a low green dish with a cluster of such shells used as a focal point, but low in the water. Many shells have purple or a hint of lavender about them and these give a wonderful pearly effect to water.

Then there are the larger shells, some big enough to make containers for miniature arrangements. Before you use a shell for flowers test it to make sure at what angle it is best stood. Sometimes the slightest tilt the wrong way may cause it to empty quickly. This done, you can hold the shell firmly on its base by pressing a tiny pill of either Plasticine or Oasisfix at the point where it rests. And, by the way, another shell either flat or upturned can often be used as a base. Press the shell down firmly, just as you do a pinholder, and it should stay in place as you want it thanks to the adhesive pill.

If you should find it impossible to stand the shell so that it retains enough water for the flowers, fill it instead with crumbs of well-soaked Florapak or Oasis. Once the flowers are arranged in this, keep them well sprayed. Of course, if you use the shells as containers for little dried flowers water will present no problem. Dry Oasis pushed into the shell and left protruding from the aperture a little way will simplify arrangement.

I like large, barnacle-encrusted shells and I find these extremely decorative when grouped at the base of tall, leafless stems. They are helpful also when you are looking for materials to provide contrasts of textures. Rough oyster shells, the bigger the better, ought never to be passed by! If you eat the oysters in a restaurant, ask for a wrapper in which to take the shells home.

All of these things will be salty and should be well washed several times in fresh water before they are used with flowers, some of which will dislike the slightest trace of salt and will die if they receive it.

Seaweed too has its uses. Long dried ribbons of thong weed can be found lying on the sand up above the high-water mark. Some may already be twisted in the right fashion for you. Others may need re-designing. The weed can be softened by soaking it in water and once it is pliable you can curve it in the way you want. Lay it on a piece of paper to dry again. If you want deep, definite curves, it might be best to tie the thong weed, or alternatively to use clothes pegs to clip one portion to another. Once dried the weed will retain its shape. You can alter it again some other time if you wish. Such pieces are useful in giving line to an arrangement.

I use thong weed to fashion long 'lazy S' lines or Hogarth curves. These are fun with uniform flowers, especially if these grow on very straight stems. Such flowers lend themselves ideally to stylized, modern designs. Try, for instance, making a long S of weed (this is usually best done in two parts, one rising from the container, one flowing down) and arranging moon daisies or mayweed to run parallel with the S. I have used this theme often in large shell containers when I have been arranging all kinds of summer flowers, both wild and cultivated, including on one occasion the garden rose Summer Holiday. I couldn't resist this, it seemed a natural!

These long pieces of seaweed often have the sucker-like root still attached and sometimes the effect is more interesting if this end is used as the tip. Naturally it all depends upon the other components in the arrangement.

Pieces of wrack can be separated and reassembled to make a sea fan to be used as a frame or background to certain kinds of arrangements. Some of the daintier pinks, blush-brown and red seaweeds which you find in rock pools can be dried and used in pictures or other types of perpetuelle decorations.

The best way to deal with these is to carry them home still moist and once there float them in a bowl of water so that they open out prettily, then slip a piece of paper under them so that the weed is spread out on it and lift it out. A knitting needle helps to separate one branch from another should they overlap too much. Once the paper and the seaweed have dried the weed can be pressed.

If you have ever seen driftwood on sale you will know that this is some of the most valuable jetsam you can discover. I have pieces galore, all found on some shore or another. It is of many shapes and sizes, but all of the same sand-sun-sea-wind-induced smoothness. Often it is difficult to decide from what plant the wood originated.

One seldom finds driftwood just lying around unless, that is, you happen on an unfrequented beach not far from trees or near a river mouth. It has to be sought, even dug or mined! You often find a small portion projecting above the sand, and one glance is usually sufficient to determine whether or not it is attached to a likely piece. The only way to be quite sure is to start digging.

I once found a lovely piece, roughly spoonshaped, with its bowl large enough to hold either cut flowers or growing plants. I line it with a piece of thick polythene when I want to use it for this purpose.

Sometimes the bark still covers portions of the driftwood. If it has been weathered sufficiently it is quite easy to prise this off, even with a thumbnail. If the bark holds tight, however, don't make the mistake of scraping it off, for the marks will show and you will sacrifice the natural smoothness which is the major part of the great beauty of driftwood. Take it home and soak it in rainwater until the bark comes away without difficulty.

Driftwood is used in flower arrangement in a number of ways, mainly to give a definite line to a design. It is used to great effect in arrangements that have no blooms in them but are composed of leaves, fruits of all kinds including seed heads, and indeed entire plants. Such decorations can be very beautiful indeed (*see* Pls. I, 1).

Perpetuelles also blend well with driftwood, as you would expect. It is possible to plan arrangements of this type so that the driftwood forms the base or container as well as part of the perpetuelle group. Often you can find flat pieces to which the sea has given a new and individual appearance. These make good bases on which to mount a piece which is curved or gnarled. Use a powerful adhesive or screw one to the other. Be sure to cover the underside of the base, especially if there is a screw head in it.

I often use driftwood to help me to anchor difficult-to-position stems. Sometimes you will find pieces which are two-pronged like the old-fashioned dolly pegs. When I want to arrange a branch at an angle that calls for some pressure on the stem where it leaves the container, I 'hairpin' it with a piece of driftwood of this nature. Being driftwood and attractive it is not necessary to hide it. Indeed, sometimes I arrange more at this point and bring the driftwood in as an integral part of the arrangement.

Slender pieces, or those which taper conveniently, can be arranged just as you would any tall branch, with shorter materials grouped around or before it. Sometimes you can position it quite easily, pushing the end down through wire-netting, or by impaling it on a pinholder, but often it is both too thick and too tough for this and you will have to fit a foot onto it so that it will stand firmly. This can be done quite simply by nailing or screwing two pieces of baton, crosswise, onto the base.

When I want a long piece of driftwood to flow out from a container at a certain angle which I find cannot be achieved by arranging it in the normal manner, I mount the driftwood on 18-gauge florist wire, sometimes using more than one length if the wood is heavy or very thick. I bend the wire or wires into a U, then at a point in the wood where it will leave the container, the wire straddles it, leaving equal legs on each side. These are then twisted once or twice around each other so that the driftwood is held tight in the loop and the two pegs are brought close together to form a single stem. This is pushed down into the container, through the netting or other type of stem-holder, and the driftwood can then be arranged as required. The exception to this is that when the wood seems unbalanced or top-heavy it is best not to bring the two legs together but to insert them apart. Before now, when a piece of wood has been particularly difficult to persuade to stay put, I have twisted these wire legs around the wire-netting near the rim of the container. By pressing or bending on the mount wires you can make the driftwood stay as you want it.

Larger, thicker pieces look well used low down in arrangements. Cunningly done it can appear that the flowers are growing from the wood.

I like to use three or sometimes more small chunky pieces (I only collect those which have interesting shapes) placed together in such a way that they look like one twisted or gnarled piece. As a rule these are quite easy to use. Being in sections one can lay them on a rim or among stems without any other special method of support, or alternatively they can be wired in the manner previously described.

At times I place one short piece behind another in a series of steps to separate flowers of different kinds, each to its own layer. For instance, ivy trails and moss appearing to grow from the lowest step, a 'plant' of short flowers (say primroses and a little ground ivy) on the step above, taller kinds (say cow parsley) above this and a branch of oak catkins at the top like a little tree. The driftwood actually hides the containers of all of these and it is featured as much as possible. There is no point in hiding anything so attractive. A shallow container or a tray is used for a composition of this type.

Attractive wall decorations can be made by using driftwood as the container, and these can be quite large if a considerable area has to be covered. This is an exciting way to decorate a large bare wall or a door which is seldom used. As I write I can look up and admire a lovely piece of ivy driftwood, which I found in Ireland, hanging on my studio wall. The foot of this is branched and splayed so that it spans four or five inches. Flowers can be arranged at this point. To hold them you have to fix some small vessel behind the driftwood. Strong elastic bands will do to hold some. Tins can be nailed to the wood at a point quite near the rim. Even slender pieces of driftwood can be used this way and for these you can use small tablet tubes lashed behind the wood with self-adhesive tape. I have also used small plastic bags filled with well-soaked Florapak or Oasis.

It really is well worth while making a considerable collection of driftwood, because you can draw from it time and time again. The pieces will last for years.

Often I make a little 'florasculpture' with materials I find on the seashore (Pl. 2). These are grouped together following the same rules I apply to my flower arrangements. I find them satisfying to do and they are always much admired. They contain driftwood, shells, seaweeds, all marine items in as much variety in their way as there is in a mixed bunch of flowers. I use a base of wood, cork or stone. Sometimes a pinholder is used, although more frequently one item is used to support, display and enhance another.

My own designs of this nature are planned to be broken down and separated again after a time, but should I wish to give away the florasculpture this will mean that it must be transported and hence all the items in it will have to be secure. Assembly then is slower though certainly surer. I use a touch of Polyfilla to fix things to the base, and when these are anchored a few more pieces can be added. These may have to be propped up or supported as they dry. Unlike a flower arrangement one starts at the base and works upwards. When I come to the materials nearer the surface, and to tiny shells, I use a strong transparent adhesive to anchor them.

Once one leaves the seashore itself there are still many lovely things to be found. As I was writing earlier about lichen I had a mental picture of the many times I have walked near the coast and found fascinating wind-sculpted trees draped with thick shawls of grey-green lichen, covering and softening their branches.

Search below the trees first. If these are tall you may find windfallen, beautifully covered branches and you are sure to find many small pieces of lichen. These can be very useful in many small arrangements. If you make pictures of perpetuelles they will provide a texture and a hue that will be different from most of the other things. You will not need to press them.

In warm, dry interiors lichen becomes brittle. If you use it with fresh flowers spray it occasionally to keep its appearance soft and dewy. A friend of mine 'fixes' the lichen by spraying it with hairspray so that a branch will last for months and months. Another uses a clear varnish spray. Personally I do not like this because the varnish gives the lichen an uncharacteristic lustre.

The soft, hoary texture of lichen-covered branches is a beautiful foil for silky preserved leaves of beech or the leathery finished rich brown which glycerine and water gives to laurel foliage. You can make beautiful and long-lasting arrangements by mixing these with branches of larch cones and individual larger cones, used like flowers, or with conkers mounted on false stems and clusters of acorns in their cups.

I like to see such arrangements in polished brown containers. Metal, like the Britannia ware that was so popular a century or so ago, suits them well. Some people make a container by using one of the figures made from this and similar metals to hold a small vessel in some way. Quite often one of the figure's arms is raised and a tin can be firmly fastened to it. Later this becomes hidden by the arrangement. If all the materials are dried and fairly light in weight all you need to do is to fasten on a block of Oasis with Oasisfix (*see* p. 24).

Wooden containers of all kinds are perfect. You can often transform a lamp base by fitting this with a top to take water and a stem holder of some kind. I sometimes make wooden vases by wrapping a split cane mat around a large jar. Sometimes the mat is dyed to a rich, chestnut brown. There are many ways in which you can adapt things which were never originally intended to hold flowers. One friend of mine made a wooden vase from a piece of staircase banister!

Lichen branches also look well in low containers (*see* Pls. 15–17). I like lichen with pewter and I often use a deep pewter plate for a semi-permanent arrangement in which lichen is arranged in a pleasing line as the framework of the arrangement, while room is left in the foreground for fresh flowers. These are changed as they fade and replaced with fresh. For a permanent arrangement, following the same lines, try driftwood and shells.

Those who like grasses, and especially the giant ones, will find a great variety near the sea, too many in fact to list in detail. Sand dunes, salt marshes, sandy heaths and river estuaries all have their own species.

There are so many grasses, although a few of them are rare. Some of them, like the marram grass, *Ammophila arenaria*, are used to hold drifting sand, and so you will sometimes find areas where this grass has obviously been especially planted. Do not gather this, please, while it is new. Leave it to increase and knit together.

Incidentally take care when you gather tough grasses. The leaves of some have sharp edges and can cut through skin, sometimes quite deeply. It is always best to take a pair of pocket pruners or small secateurs for grass, because as well as damaging your hands you are also likely to pull up the entire plant at the roots.

Seaside plants tend to be local and I am loth to encourage any-one to gather them simply because one feels that so many people visit the coast and all should be able to enjoy the flowers and plants they see growing there. Some, like the sea lavender or statice, *Limonium vulgare*, are listed as being common in muddy salt marshes, but there are other limoniums which are rarer, and unless you are certain which is which you should let them stay.

These are everlasting flowers and the precursors of the bright statice we grow annually in our borders for winter bouquets. Also used for the same purpose is the sea holly, *Eryngium maritimum*. which likes sand and seashores. It is both very glaucous and very prickly, so much so that it needs careful handling and I prefer to pass it by. I have been hurt too often!

One of my favourite members of the great family umbelliferae grows mainly by the sea on limy soil. This is the wild carrot, *Daucus carota* (*see* Pl. XI). White and truly lacy, with a denser though not less dainty texture than most of the other Queen Anne's lace type of flowers, it looks well with the first autumn fruits. It flowers from June to August. It has tough, wiry stems which must be cut, not plucked.

When it fruits the umbels become concave and are thick, almost woolly, in appearance. If you want to dry them, the moment to pick is as soon as they begin to close and while they are still full and fluffy. Hang them upside-down to dry in some cool, dry place. They will close and look like an umbrella blown inside-out. When they are quite dry, and you are ready to use them, gently coax them open. You will find that the stems are not brittle and will respond to your coaxing. Gently push them back until you have an attractive open umbel which you can use for many kinds of dried flower arrangements.

three

Arranging Your Flowers

My earliest recollection of an arrangement of wild flowers is of a two-pound jam jar perched precariously on an outer window-sill of a neighbour's house filled with a mixture of ox-eye daisies, sorrel and what we used to call wigwam grass, *Briza minor*. The stems stood in water which had already turned green, for the flowers had not been stripped of their leaves and these were fast decaying.

Looking back, most of the wild flowers gathered by my child-hood friends finished up outside the house. Possibly this was because the petals soon dropped and the water soon stank.

The only flowers my mother banished this way was the first posy I ever picked. My father had called to see a farmer, and the two men stood talking at a gate by a little wood, and beyond, as far as I could see and carpeting the ground, were the most wonderful starry flowers. Might I pick some? I remember that the man looked amused at this request from the little girl, but he told me to take as many as I wished and I picked until my hands could hold no more. I was enchanted. I had only just come from London to live in the country and all the way home I thought of how delighted my mother was going to be with the flowers. She was, at the sight of them, but not at the smell. My posy was of wild garlic!

In spite of my remonstrances our neighbour's example was

followed and my flowers went outside in a jam jar. However, I was promised that if I found some other kind of flower I would be given a proper vase if I would arrange them myself. My mother never could find patience to arrange flowers and I never remember seeing her doing them. This little domestic task became my province.

For years the flowers I arranged were always wild ones, and as one would expect I gradually found which were the best kinds to pick and how to arrange them once I got them home.

In those days we had no kind of stem-holders except a piece of metal mesh over the top of a rose bowl, and for other low bowls a dome of glass, into which holes had been made, to stand in the centre. One inserted the flowers' stems into these, and although this type of holder was effective in one sense it was ineffective in others because, as a rule, the only way a flower would stand would be upright. The rose bowl mesh was also troublesome because, although it held the flowers in position at rim level to a certain degree, you could not position a stem with any certainty because the base of the stem would skid about on the floor of the container.

If you wanted to fill a bowl to get flowers in a semispherical shape, often the only way to do it would be first to arrange flowers or leaves all around the rim and then gradually to work your way inwards until, finally, you lowered the centre stem in place through the interlocked stems. This could be a critical moment. Sometimes all the other stems rose from the water, the mass disintegrated and one had to begin all over again.

Fortunately those days are past. Accurate stem placement today is only a matter of moments and results are guaranteed. I hope that skilled flower arrangers who may read this book will bear with me when I explain to those who are just beginning to take an interest in this subject how we ensure today that stems stay just as we want them.

The simplest and cheapest of all stem-holders is large-mesh wire-netting, sometimes called chicken-wire, because it is the kind used for hen coops. It must be the large mesh because this is so much more malleable than the small. You have to crumple or crush the netting into shape because it is as important to have it in the lower levels of a container as it is at rim level. I find that people who still have difficulty in arranging flowers easily usually do not use sufficient mesh in the container. As a general rule you should cut a piece (I use old secateurs for this because they are quicker than wire-cutters) which measures a little over twice the width of the widest diameter of the container and twice the depth. Fold this roughly into a U and then push it into the vessel, keeping the cut portion uppermost. If you find that the netting is inclined to slip a little, as it sometimes does in either highly glazed containers or in those which are wide at the rim, take some of those cut ends and hook them over the rim in three or four places to anchor the netting.

You may have to make variations on this theme according to the kind of flowers you are intending to arrange. For instance, frail, thin stems need more supporting and you may need more netting or even a smaller mesh than for thicker stems.

Quite often I use a small piece of crushed wire-netting in only one portion of a container. Suppose, for example, that I wish to make a little group of primroses, arranged much as they grow, in one corner of a large dish. I then place the netting at this one point only in the shape of a small ball. It can be anchored, should this be necessary, by first pressing a small piece of Plasticine or Oasisfix on the dry floor of the container. The netting is then pushed into this, the flowers arranged and the water added.

Sometimes it is more practical to provide a small supplementary vessel to hold a small cluster such as I have described. This can be a small food tin, perhaps a washed salmon tin, for example. This can be filled with netting and water and subsequently the flowers placed in it will hide or camouflage it.

Today plastics such as Florapak and Oasis are frequently used as stem-holders and, like so many modern inventions, make one's task much easier. Both these materials are made of some form of urea formaldehyde and can be obtained in large blocks or specially shaped smaller ones. Their advantage is that they will immediately hold stems in the way you arrange them, even upside-down! Furthermore it is not necessary to insert a great length of stem; a fraction of an inch is enough to hold some in place. You can see that this will be an advantage when you have only short flowers and wish to use them in a taller design, or if you have to arrange leaves, many of which have very short stems indeed.

Both of these stem-holders and other similar to them are water-retentive. Florapak holds water longer, but set against this is the fact that it must be inserted inside a container. Oasis on the other hand remains firm and so can be used ex-container, by which I mean that you can simply stand it on a saucer or even fix it against a wall. But moisture from Oasis evaporates quickly and so it must be inspected daily and kept sprayed or moistened in some manner.

There is one disadvantage common to both these materials and it is that it is difficult, and sometimes impossible, to insert soft, pliable and sappy stems easily. The only way to do this is first to make holes with a skewer, knitting needle or some similar object, and I think that having to bother with this rather defeats the purpose of the materials, which is to simplify arrangement.

If you are a novice, and just beginning to experiment with flower arrangement, I am sure it will not be long before you discover that it is often the best plan to combine one or more stem-holders. I find that I do this most when I am arranging a mixture of flowers. In this case I place one of the foamed stem-holders at the base of the vessel, perhaps to half fill it, and into this I lightly press the wire-netting to reach as far as the rim or perhaps even above it for a little way. I find then that strong, straight, firm stems can go through the netting and be instantly held as I want them by the foamed stem-holder below. The netting solves the problem of arranging soft or sappy stems because these are simply pushed through the layers of mesh. Water is poured in to just below rim level and kept topped up daily.

The methods I have just described are for containers deep enough to hide all evidences of stem-holders, for these are not pretty things. But what happens when you want to arrange, say, a single branch rising from a low bowl? In this case the best holder to use is a pinholder. The stems are impaled on its pinpoints at any angle according to the way the arranger wants them

Here again I find that it sometimes suits me best to combine pinholder and wire-netting when I am using materials which differ considerably in the thickness and texture of their stems.

Although the pinholders are heavy they may still have to be anchored in position. This is simply done by fixing little washers of Plasticine or Oasisfix on the under surface. There are two points to remember about this. The first is that surfaces of both pinholder and container must be bone dry or the clays will not stick, and of course the clay itself must be dry. All you need are three, four or five pea-sized pills according to the size of the pinholder. Press these around the circumference of the pinholder firmly but lightly so they are not flattened. Now press this down hard in the required position so that the pills are flattened. It should now hold so firmly that even if you turn the container upside-down it will stay in place. Once it is anchored you can arrange even the heaviest stems with confidence, although, naturally, you should choose a pinholder of size suitable to the subjects you intend to use. For this reason try to get an assortment of sizes and vary the shapes too. You can get rectangular kinds as well as round and crescent pinholders. Sometimes you will need more than one for an arrangement. If you are a handyman you may be able to make some yourself.

I use low containers with pinholders quite a lot, for by using them I find that I can place the stems so that they follow a natural line and appear to flow easily. So often one finds an attractively shaped branch which calls out to be arranged against a bare plain wall so that it can be admired. When I do this I often complete the arrangement by bringing into the design or composition a few other things I have found near by, to make an ecological pattern, one might say.

These arrangements become living picture stories, and I find that everyone who sees them appreciates and enjoys them. Think how easily you can tell a little story of springtime this way. The branch can rise from the water like a lovely leaning tree. The holder itself must be hidden, and to do this both effectively and attractively you can use mossy stones, or you may be lucky enough to find an early root of daisy or celandine in flower, with perhaps a trail or two of ground ivy. These, with fern-like moss, can be made to appear to grow at the foot of the tree on a little island in the water.

Alternatively, at some other time of the year perhaps, you may find a lovely bare branch, some burned gorse or perhaps a piece of driftwood or sun-bleached ivy stem from an old wall. You can create a harmony of wood using plant materials that have woody textures, such as dried oyster fungus, cones, bark, gleaming conkers and brown, leathery leaves. An arrangement such as this can last for months.

You will find that the way you hide the pinholder can be an important part of the arrangement. Not only stones but also flowers and leaves can be used to conceal it. Small pieces of driftwood, shells and fungi are some of the other materials which can be used.

Often, and especially if you use a fairly large trough, you will want to group certain little flowers as though they were growing some distance away from the main portion of the arrangement. It is possible to buy tiny pinholders for this purpose, small and dainty enough to take a few stems and which in holding these become quite hidden, so that it appears that the flowers rise up from the water unaided.

I use circles of metal to hold these groups in place, even a serviette ring is suitable at times. Small lengths of lead can be curved to whatever shape and size you want. If you should find a small stone or rock with one or more holes right through it, save it for arrangements of this kind.

When I want to arrange just one lovely branch in a taller vase I often use a pinholder fixed right down on the floor of the container. This I do particularly when I can see that I shall want to pull and coax the branch so that it stands out of the vertical. At other times, and this depends to a great extent on the character and shape of the container, I might use a little wire-netting wedged firmly in the lower part of the container where it will not show. This is when I know that the surface of the water will show in the finished arrangement. When a fairly slim container is used it is sometimes unnecessary to have a stem-holder of any kind. All you have to do is bend, snap, but not sever, the base of the branch so that it forms a foot, like the lower part of the letter L. The length of this foot should be exactly the same as the diameter of the base, so that when you insert it the foot will fit snugly across the container and hold the branch in place.

Branches of all kinds, whether they be early catkins, late autumnal coloured beech or even preserved leaves, can be used as long-lasting frameworks for arrangements with flowers whose lives are more fleeting.

Of course containers for flowers are important, but these should not be just vessels that hold water: they should also be a part of the arrangement. There are some people who think that wild flowers should go only in unsophisticated vessels, in earthenware pitchers, hand-thrown pottery or stone jars. This is a matter of personal taste. I think that it depends mainly on where the flowers are to stand as well as on the type of flowers. My wild flower arrangements come in all styles, from the very simple and uncalculated to the most sophisticated of party decorations.

As a rule I find that people who have not done a great deal of flower arrangement, and this applies especially to children, tend to use containers which are really too large for the flowers they hold.

Flowers ought to be able to stand free and not be dominated by the vessel that contains them. The whole point of arrangement, as opposed to merely putting flowers in water, is that the flowers are displayed in such a way that you can admire them and see each one clearly.

Many people cut flowers with stems far too short. It is true that many stems have to be shortened for arrangement, for it is not easy to arrange stems of similar length in a pleasing pattern, but if you have always to begin with all short stems you will find that the styles of arrangement you can choose become very limited.

However, there are many little wild plants which have both short stems and tiny flowers. Sometimes, taken alone, these flowers are not really very distinctive. But unity is strength, even where flowers and colour are concerned. If when these types of flowers are gathered each species is made into a little posy, heads all at one level, they can then be treated as though they were a single, short-stemmed and quite colourful large bloom.

The colours of these posied flowers can often be accentuated by arranging a collar of some foliage, either harmonizing or contrasting, around the outer edge. Ivy, always so plentiful everywhere, seems a natural choice, although sometimes the texture of the leaves is a little too thick for the delicate blooms of some of the softer-leaved weeds. Instead of ivy try collars of such leaves as the ferny herb Robert and other geraniums, both wild and barren strawberries, wood potentilla, wood sorrel and the largest leaves of the prettily lobed ground ivy.

If you have patience enough to make several posies of each kind of flower they can be used effectively in various ways. Laid alternately around the rim of a shallow dish, deep soup plate or shallow fruit bowl, they can make a ring of posies.

Dishes which are a little too deep can be made more accommodating by filling them to the brim with crumpled soft paper, peat, crumbled Florapak or Oasis, sand or wire-netting, all hidden by a layer of green moss, the surface of which should be about an inch below the rim. Fill the dish with water so that everything is well soaked and arrange the posies by resting them on this moist bed. They will remain fresh and dewy this way, and you can help them last even longer by spraying them, preferably with an atomizer, mainly the leaves and stems, with clean water on occasion.

Collared posies look surprisingly sophisticated placed in a ring around the base of a candle which has been fixed first onto a warmed pinholder stood in the centre of a plate or shallow round dish. They look lovely when grouped at the foot of some well-shaped branch of early blossom: young, ruby-coloured, newly opened larch cones, unfolding sticky buds, lichen-covered hawthorn or a piece of gorse root or suitable driftwood.

I like also to make them tower one above the other to make either a pillar or sometimes a long thick curve of flowers. One can do this by using either a series of tablet tubes or alternatively portions of thick, hollow hogweed or similar stems, each large enough to take a posied stem. The hogweed stem portions can be fixed on a pinholder, but they must be filled with water as well as stood in it. The tubes are a little more difficult to position this way, but you will have no difficulty if you use a block of well-soaked Oasis instead. The tubes need not be inserted in the top portion only, but can lean out from the sides if this aids the design.

If you want a rule to follow for flower arrangement, possibly the most helpful deals with height and proportion of the tallest stem in the arrangement. If you ensure that this, measured from the point where it is seen at the rim, is at least one and a half times the height of the container, your flowers will never look squat or subdued.

This is only a general guide, because obviously one must always adapt arrangement to suit the setting as well as the flowers. For instance, if you have gathered a bunch of ox-eye daisies that you want to set on a low table, so that you see them most frequently below eye level, they will look attractive stood, posy fashion, though not with their stems tied together, in a tankard or some similar container. My advice there would be to choose a container which is roughly half the height of the flowers, so that they can spread out a little with sufficient room to grow and breathe.

All year through some of the loveliest arrangements can be made from foliage, with few if any true blooms. You can use seeding stems, umbels, immature green fruits and berries, mature green-black ivy berries in winter, grasses and ferns in all green arrangements. These have the advantage of blending with almost any interior colour design and they can look both unsophisticated and elegant. But foliage arrangements can also be extraordinarily colourful. You will find many individual leaves or branches of foliage which are as vivid as any flower. In autumn and through winter there are many berries, including the bright holly.

If you are new to flower arrangement, and want to try your

hand at a large arrangement of this kind, go first to the lovely beech. This grows in a most obliging manner so far as the flower arranger is concerned. A side branch is usually well shaped, roughly triangular in outline, all ready to be set at the back of the arrangement to act as a framework for the other materials (*see* Pl. 24). Cut one a little larger than you really need so that you can trim it if necessary.

Put this tallest stem in position first, right against the rim of the container. You will then be left with plenty of space for the other stems in front. Let this first tall stem define the height and general style of the decoration, with long side-stems if you want it spreading, shorter ones if you want a tall, slimmer line.

Beech grows flat with side-branches going only two ways, so that there is little trimming of branches to be done. Simply cut off damaged leaves and any clusters which overlap each other so much that the effect is too dense. Remember that there are many more leaves to follow.

If you use individual stems at the back of an arrangement, their tips can sketch the outline for you the same way as the beech. Once again, try to get these as near to the rim at the back as you can. If you are making a symmetrical arrangement let the centre stem be taller than the others and try to make these roughly equal on each side of it. Work from the tip, downwards to the centre rim, finishing up there with materials flowing over it and outwards from left to right. Do not attempt to arrange one side or the whole centre portion first and then turn to the sides. If you do you will have difficulty in inserting later stems and will have the greatest difficulty in getting a balanced result.

Once I have decided on the shape and the style I usually follow the bent of the flowers as I pick them out from the bucket in which they have been hardened, rather than turn them all over to look for the right piece for a particular place. Those that curve naturally to the right or left are set on that side of the arrangement. If, while I am supposedly working on the top area, I should find a piece that is perfect for the lower zones it goes in place there and then.

As you would expect, I employ lots of little tricks of the trade. The best way I know of getting a little branch to flow over the rim of a container in an attractive and natural way is to cut it with a portion of its main stem still attached. This portion, quite often at right angles to its lateral, goes down into the vase leaving the entire lateral on view. This is the method I adopt also when making low arrangements in which I want a stem to, say, lean out over the water, or perhaps to curve around a taller stem.

You will find that there are many ways in which you can make the actual materials you use work for you.

Stems I arrange are often much higher than one and a half times the height of the container. I like to take one great branch and have it as tall as I can. My cottage ceilings are low, so I sometimes stand the container on a low table, sometimes even on the floor.

This rule is helpful when you are following a fairly formal and symmetrical pattern, such as when the flowers are being arranged in a vase set against the wall, their tips following the outlines of a circle, oval or triangle.

So far as wild flowers are concerned, I think that the beginner in arrangement can learn a great deal from the plants themselves. Primroses, for instance, look best when they are arranged on a low dish to look a little like a growing plant; cow parsley is most elegant and looks most at home when its long stems are arranged to rise up from a mass of its own leaves; branches of all kinds can be made to follow the shape of the tree's outline, the container playing the role of the tree trunk.

A guide I use and one which I find so helpful is one of the rules from the ancient classical Japanese style: that the tip of the tallest curved stem should always be over the centre of the base of the container. Try this out for yourself. Take a curved branch and stand it upright and study the effect. Then slowly move it until the tip is over the centre of the base. I am sure you will see a transformation!

Candlesticks are often used as flower-holders and in this case they are fitted with a candle cup, a little bowl with a leg, candle-thick, which fits into the well made for the candle. When flowers are arranged in the bowl or cup some stems are brought low to hide it. I use these cups also to fit into the necks of bottles and other narrow-necked containers.

four

Preparing Your Flowers

How you gather flowers and how you look after them once they are taken from the plant is extremely important, for this concerns not only the lasting qualities of the flowers themselves but also the wellbeing of the plant on which they grow.

Anyone who gathers wild flowers is almost certain to have to transport them for some distance, often quite a long way from the point where they were found growing. Do remember that it is always unwise, even selfish, to pick any at all unless you can ensure that they will arrive home little the worse for their journey. Unless you can be certain of this it is best to leave them alone. This applies particularly in late spring onwards, when the weather is hot and sunny. How often one sees discarded bunches of bluebells and other flowers, obviously thrown aside because they had wilted in some hot hand. It also applies to the maturity of the material, but more of this later.

The thing that kills flowers on these occasions is loss of moisture. When this occurs the flowers or plants first wilt and then, when they have lost too much of their moisture, they begin to shrivel, and once this happens no amount of first-aid, care or treatment can revive them. So the first thing one has to do is to ensure that from the moment they are picked they remain as fresh, turgid and moisture-filled as possible. As there is seldom opportunity to replace the moisture they are losing at this stage, obviously the next best thing is to try to prevent excessive loss of moisture, fortunately a comparatively simple thing to do nowadays.

Take with you a collection of polythene bags, large, roomy ones for long, wide and bulky stems, and a series of smaller bags for short-stemmed subjects, leaves, moss and lichen. I find that fungi are best placed on moss or earth in a covered tin or a plastic food box with lid. The exception are those fungi which are to be dried and these can begin their drying process on the journey. Simply place them on newspaper in an open container. I always keep a few containers of different sorts in the car in case I find some flowers on my travels.

All these containers should be large enough to ensure that once the plant material is inside them there will remain a good layer of air between them and the top of the bag, or alternatively the lid, as well as space immediately around them. After you have put the materials in the bag—and do not crowd them—blow into it to inflate it and then close the top securely. The air around the contents will protect and cushion them.

Flowers and other plant materials which are packed dry are less likely to become damaged. Once petals and leaves become turgid by being stood in water they can easily get bruised, even by resting on each other. So your flowers will come to no harm because they have not been given a drink. Neither will they lose much of the moisture present in their cells, because inside the bag their rate of respiration is slowed down and they will keep fresh inside for several hours.

Should the materials be wet when they are gathered you would be wise first to swish them dry and then cover them. Placed wet inside bags or boxes they are liable to become spoiled should the weather or the conditions during transport be warm or sunny.

In a book I once wrote on commercial flower marketing I observed that the best packing material for a flower is another flower. Don't make the mistake of padding flowers with damp moss or paper. Simply pick and bunch them and get them into covers as quickly as you can.

It is a good plan to pick and pack certain kinds together rather than make mixtures, simply because the flowers have to receive treatment and become properly hardened once you get them home, and the quicker you can get them into water, the less you have to handle them, the better. It is much easier to lift out a bunch of, say, moon daisies, one of grasses and another of bugle, in which all the stems are roughly of one length and the flower heads are level, and stand each of these in a suitable vessel of water, than it is to have to select and grade the stem lengths of a mixed bunch when the flowers (and you, perhaps!) are tired and should be drinking and becoming refreshed. Several small bunches can go in one large bag should this be necessary, although I find it easier in the long run to keep them separate, each in its own container.

When you pack flowers put them in the bag stem ends first, and either stand the bag in a cardboard box, a basket or a bucket, or if you are travelling by car even hang the bag, so that the weight of the plant material rests on the stem ends and not on the blooms.

Leaves are easily placed one on another, spoon fashion. This makes a nice compact bunch and it also prevents them from becoming damaged. Branches of flat, growing foliage such as beech can also be laid one on the other.

Should you be gathering only a few flowers, possibly a mixture, it is a good plan to use a branch of beech as a backing and to lay the flowers on this, putting the long ones at the back of the sheaf with the short-stemmed kinds in the front. You will be able to slip this inside a bag and either carry it with the cool beech on your arm taking the weight of the flowers, or lay it flat on the seat or floor of the car.

Try to prevent the sun shining directly on the flowers while you are transporting them. Even a sheet of newspaper laid over the bags will help to shade them, and if you can make this damp it will also keep the air cool.

Having done all you can to keep the flowers comfortable and fresh on their journey back to your home, the next thing is to make sure that they are properly conditioned or hardened, that is, taking water correctly, before you attempt to arrange them.

Cut plant materials of all kinds give off moisture from their entire surfaces, yet they take it up through their cut stems ends only. Often they cannot take up moisture as quickly as they are losing it and when this happens they wilt, even though stems are in water. This is the reason one recommends giving flowers and foliage a deep drink before arranging them. This entails standing the stems in water as deep as possible without actually immersing the blooms. The deeper the water the better so far as the conditioning process is concerned. Once the stems and leaves are turgid almost all flowers can be arranged in shallow containers if you wish.

By putting leafy stems under water while the water is being conducted to the blooms we prevent the moisture from being lost from any surface and ensure that it is quickly conveyed to the petals. Once these are turgid, and you can easily see when they are, you can be sure that the vessels in the stems which convey the water to all parts of the plant are working properly. Usually once this happens there are no further problems. But sometimes, even after they have had a long, deep drink, you may arrange certain flowers only to find that they are still wilting badly. This is frequently the case with blossom, which has a lot of immature foliage on the same stem and with branches of young leaves. The soft leaves continue to release their moisture too quickly, and the trouble is that not only do they wilt but the blossom wilts also. To prevent this happening almost all blossom has to have a great proportion of its foliage cut away. Unfortunately this often takes away some of the character of the blossom, and if you particularly want to have foliage as well in most cases you would be well advised to harden this and arrange it separately. Often it is enough to remove just some of the foliage and let a few of the smaller leaves remain.

There are several ways one can help the stems to take up water quickly, and one or other of these methods should be used when branched of young or immature (but often beautifully coloured) foliage is to be conditioned. One is always to split the stem ends of any but very soft and sappy materials. This has become second nature with me, and I find myself doing it automatically whenever I place any woody stem in water to harden it. By doing this we expose the inner tissues of the stem and we also help to expel any air bubble that may be present. When we pick or cut a stem we interrupt the flow of moisture up the stem and an air-lock frequently forms. When one of these is present the water just cannot travel past it. This is why it is sometimes a good plan to re-cut a wilting stem at a point higher up the stem, thus by-passing the air-lock. If you cut the stem under water you can often actually see the air bubble as it is expelled.

Of course it is likely that when you come to arrange the materials you will want to re-cut the stems, and sometimes a split stem is a nuisance to arrange because it is not easy to push it through the wire-netting or some other stem-holder. In this case you simply cut the stem on a long slant, for this also exposes a greater area of the inner tissue and allows it to absorb moisture with greater speed.

Sometimes, even after all this, the lovely branch of young foliage, say bronzed, silky maple, will not perk up as it should. When this is the case the leaves themselves need immersing, either in a deep bucket or even by laying them in a bath of water for at least an hour. Some people begin by immersing young foliage in cold water and after an hour they split the stem ends and stand them in hot water for a while. Both methods are effective. Another method is to keep the foliage in its cover bag while the stems are drinking.

You may have noticed that sometimes after apparently fresh and turgid flowers have been arranged they have wilted inexplicably. You can avoid this happening by always using tepid water for the flowers' first drink. As a matter of fact I use it also when I am arranging them, because so often the stems have to be re-cut and I think that it is a wise precaution.

I use tepid water for conditioning all types, but it must be only tepid, about 21° C. If it is too hot it will damage the leaves and the stems.

Hotter water can be used for other purposes. When very woody or fibrous stems are to be conditioned it is best to split the stem ends and then stand them in about two or three inches of boiling water. They should then be left until the water cools. After this they can be arranged in fresh water and, as I said earlier, it is wise to use tepid water when you fill the container.

Some daisies will not take water properly, not even tepid water. The best way to condition these is to stand their stem ends in boiling water also.

Poppies and all the euphorbias and others which exude a milky latex when cut must have their stem ends singed to stop this exudation before they can take water. Simply hold the stem ends over a candle flame or gas jet until they blacken and then stand them in tepid water. Re-singe if you re-cut.

People sometimes ask me if there are some flowers which kill others if they are arranged together. I honestly don't think there are, but what does happen is that some flowers cause the water to become foul more quickly than others and this poisons all. It is important to strip the end portion of the stems which are to go under water. If any foliage remains on these it will quickly decompose and make the water impure and perhaps even toxic.

It is not a good plan to change the water daily, neither is it good, as I have sometimes seen recommended, to take out the flowers and re-cut their stem ends. My goodness! The time one would have to spend in doing the flowers, apart from anything else. Keep the water topped up daily. Use rainwater if possible. Keep containers clean and wash them thoroughly after use. Avoid standing glass containers in the sun because this increases bacterial activity in the water.

Some leaves decompose more quickly than others. Daisies of all kinds are defaulters in this respect and even small pieces of leaf remaining on the stem after stripping will soon turn slimy. It is worth while adding a few pieces of charcoal to the water. These will absorb noxious gases.

It is important to keep the water as free from bacteria as possible, at least the kinds which turn it green and smelly, and there are ways to do this apart from those just mentioned. Putting a copper coin in the water really does seem to slow down this process as does using copper and other metal containers. An aspirin has the same effect.

On a hot day I often take a large arrangement, in either a tall vase or a shallow container, to the sink and there let the cold tap run hard into it, forcing stale water out and bringing in fresh water which is well aerated because of the force of the jet used.

It is important to feed flowers and I find that in winter and early spring especially, when branches are being forced open indoors, a little sustenance helps them to last very much longer and also seems to give leaves and blossom a better colour. To feed them use a small lump of sugar, a level teaspoon of glucose or a quarter of a teaspoon of honey to each pint of water. Soluble plant foods such as House Plant Plus and Baby Bio also help all kinds of shrub and tree materials. Certain other proprietary products, such as Crysal, appear to help flowers last longer and there are many commercial exhibitors who swear by them. I find they are as effective with wild flowers as they are with the mass-produced kinds. I have long used Gregory's Rose Nutrient for many kinds of flowers and plants other than roses and found it most helpful. Like so many of the others, I understand it is composed largely of glucose and certain bacteria inhibitors.

Sometimes after an arrangement has been completed it will be noticed that a pool of water has formed at the foot of the container. This is caused by water being siphoned by one of the components of the arrangement. Usually this is a leaf or some portion of a leaf which is both in the water and protruding over the rim of the container, but sometimes a downy stem which acts as a wick causes a siphon too. The water travels up the leaf or stem hairs and falls from them. Sometimes almost every drop of water from the container can be drawn away in this manner.

Search around the rim for a leaf or stem which is wet and either ease it out of position away from contact with water and the edge of the container or even remove it completely, usually the best course of action.

Always make sure that all lower leaves, especially those which have been immersed during the hardening period, are free from surface water as they are arranged. Spraying with an atomizer should not cause siphons.

Earlier I said that the wellbeing of the plant itself can depend on the way you cut your flowers, and if you have ever seen a stripped pussy willow, its bark hanging in tattered ribbons, or if you were to come along some of the lanes near my cottage with me and see how greedy people have disfigured and in some cases almost killed the hollies in the hedgerows, you will understand my feeling. Few things, in fact, should be picked. Most need to be cut, either with a sharp knife or with a pair of good secateurs. Someone gave me a neat pair of these, small enough to carry in a handbag or a pocket. Several firms now make small pocket pruners neat enough to slip into a coat pocket when you go for a walk. Wise arrangers will try to keep a pair in the glove box of a car.

On one walk we sometimes take I always come back with a bunch of foliage, even though I have plenty of my own in the garden. This is because we walk along a public footpath which today is seldom used and seems to get a little more overgrown each year. However, with the secateurs the way is kept defined because I pick those branches which grow over the pathway.

When you are looking for material it is usually so easy to pick that which is in most peril of being trampled on, run over or broken by either vehicles or pedestrians.

But there is more to flower-gathering than picking tree or shrub material. Take such little flowers as primroses, for example: why pick every one you see? And why pick all the flowers from one plant? If you want a bunch, take just one or two from each of several plants. You will make better arrangements from a few flowers than from many, and you will leave some for others to enjoy and some to seed and so propagate the very flowers you admired so much.

I am reminded of an occasion in France recently. We had driven to the top of Mont d'Or in the country near Clermont Ferrand. The way was sweet, lined with wild flowers of so many species all the way, and although it was June we enjoyed the spring flowers too as we climbed higher and higher near the snow which still lay on the mountain tops. Suddenly we were driving between fields of white narcissi. Imagine then our joy to find at the top of the mountain the ground yellow with daffodils. But it wasn't yellow for long. If we had been an hour later we would never have seen them. Three people had picked so many they could hardly hold them as they walked smiling triumphantly, and I must confess happily, back to their car. Few other people were going to see that mountain living up to its name. On the other hand, the mere fact that the flowers were there that year indicated that regardless of depredations of this kind they would grow again and cover the hillside next year.

But one of the most important things still remains to be said. Most of the flowers that are gathered would have been best left where they were growing simply because at the very time they were taken they had passed their best and were beginning to die, their work done.

Commercial growers have at last discovered that the wrong time for them to gather and market their perfect blooms is while they are at their best. More and more flowers are now reaching our markets in bud or in as young a condition as practical. This means that the customer and not the grower can watch and enjoy the flowers as they develop towards maturity, getting thereby longer life and greater glory from the blooms. We can do much the same with our wild flowers.

There are a few, both wild and cultivated, which will not continue to grow in water, and there are some which cannot take water if they are too immature. But in the main most flowers are best when cut young. By young I mean before they have been pollinated, for once pollination takes place they begin to fade. Take bluebells, our demonstration flower: if you gather these when all the bells are open you cannot expect them to last longer than a day or two before the lowest bells begin to droop and blacken. It is best to gather them when only the first bell has opened. They will then travel better and last longer.

You will find in the coming chapters that from time to time I have dealt with this question of maturity in flowers, giving a guide wherever possible. Here it will probably suffice to say that if in doubt look for the pollen. If this is ripe, if petals are dusty with it, if the centre of a daisy is dusky yellow with no green centre still to expand, the flowers are simply not worth picking. They are on their way to making seed. Let them stay to do so and remember to visit them a little earlier another year!

Often from a distance a branch or a group of flowers will look beautiful, but closer inspection may reveal that those lovely leaves have been attacked by insects and hardly a good one remains on the branch. In some seasons you can search tree after tree without ever finding a branch perfect enough to take home and enjoy.

On the other hand sometimes only one or two leaves are damaged, unfortunately often at the tips, although these can sometimes be cut away without spoiling the appearance of the whole branch. I think that grooming is very important. Personally I cannot enjoy looking at plant materials which are disfigured, and leaving aside the aesthetics of the case there is also the purely practical side. I have many house plants and so I am not anxious to import any insect or pest which might transfer its attentions to them.

It surprises me how often damaged leaves and flowers escape one's notice, so after I have finished an arrangement I always spend a little time being really critical and looking hard for faults. A groomed arrangement keeps its fresh look much longer than one in which spoiled materials have been allowed to remain.

five

Dried
and Preserved
Materials

You can capture summer and create lovely souvenirs of walks and days in the country or holidays by the sea by making dried arrangements which will last all winter through and for even longer than this should you wish. Many people who annually preserve autumn foliage for winter decoration leave it at that, but there are many more parts of plants than foliage which are well worth collecting. These can be either dried or preserved, and extending the first process they can be pressed or simply arranged and allowed to dry slowly in situ.

Such materials are extremely varied, and arrangements made from them have great beauty when they are skilfully assembled.

You can begin quite early in the year, gradually building up a collection of many kinds of things to arrange later, a pleasant way to spend the dreary days of winter. Or perhaps you might like to do as I do and wait until late summer and gradually build up a large arrangement for some special place in your home, school or place of work, treating it rather as though it were a painting, bringing home a few things from each expedition, a fallen branch of larch cones, a group of bulrushes, some beautifully pendent reeds, tall, graceful stems of nipplewort, an oak branch, some fungi, a few lovely fallen leaves, for example, all materials which need no special treatment but which can be arranged straight away. Finally, you can go out looking just for one or two special things to complete your 'painting', and when it is completed it will stand, a delightful and unusual decoration, to remind you of so many enjoyable hours.

Since more people preserve leaves than anything else, a word about these first of all.

As a general rule most branches with smooth, tough leaves can be preserved successfully, while those with rough ones such as hazel do not seem to respond so well. Usually the thicker and tougher the leaf the more dramatic the change. Do not confuse rough with downy, because many downy-leaved materials can be preserved. The lovely whitebeam, for instance, will turn a deep brown on the surface yet will retain the characteristic silvery-white downy undersides of the leaves. Tall spires of woolly verbascum will retain their fluffiness yet change their hue, taking on interesting tans under the silver-grey.

Many evergreens (although we have not many which are wild) can be preserved, and their leaves will change to varying hues of tan and deep brown.

Beech seems to be the most popular foliage of all for preserving, yet oak, hornbeam, birch and others preserve well. Sycamore does sometimes. One of the loveliest of preserved materials is wild clematis, popularly known as old man's beard.

It is well worth experimenting a little each year because a great deal seems to depend on the season. The important thing is not to leave it too late to gather the branches, otherwise the leaves will fall while they are in the preserving solution. As a matter of fact you can begin preserving beech as early as late July, and the earlier you gather and preserve the leaves the deeper the colour they become. Green beech gathered in summer ends up the colour of dull copper beech. Preserved much later it becomes a golden tan.

It is important to realize that there comes a point, just before the fall, when the leaves stop taking up water from the stems. This is why when you have gathered some attractive branches you later find that even though they have been stood in water, or perhaps a preserving fluid, they have simply curled. You cannot really gather them too soon once the summer is over, but you can certainly and easily gather them too late.

If you want autumn-tinted foliage after preservation, do as I do and watch the trees. Often you will find that one branch changes colour long before the rest of the tree. This is the moment to gather branches from that particular tree.

Branches or stems which are to be preserved have first to be conditioned. Split the stem ends and stand them in warm or hot water. Let them stay all night. Not only will this start the process of water flowing up through the stems, but it will give you the opportunity of learning if there are any branches which are too advanced to take water, and these can be discarded before you spend time and preserving fluid on them.

For the solution use one-third glycerine and two-thirds boiling water. I used to boil the two together, but someone pointed out to me that this could be dangerous, and I mention it now in case some young reader might be tempted to take an easy route to mixing the two liquids.

Stems need to be stood in about two inches of this solution, so obviously a slim container looks to be the most economical, but the drawback to this is that it will easily tilt over because of the weight or the height and width of the material it holds. For this reason I use tall tins to hold the solution and stand these inside empty buckets or other larger vessels, these being high enough and wide enough to support the branches whichever way they may care to lean.

Mix the two liquids together well and quickly and pour the solution into the containers over the ends of the stems so that they get the full impact while it is still hot.

After a few days you will be able to trace the progress of the glycerine through the veins of the leaves, which will become silkier and oilier in appearance. When it is obvious that the solution extends over the whole of the surface of the leaves remove the branches from the solution. If they are left in too long a sticky mess begins to exude from the leaf surfaces.

Once you have removed the branches they can be arranged out of water right away. If you wish to keep them for use at some later date pack them away, one carefully laid on another in boxes, or hung up stems downwards in polythene bags.

You can arrange them in water with fresh materials if you wish. Often you will find that after being placed in water the stem ends rot, and if you want to avoid this slip them into narrow plastic bags deep enough to cover the portion which will go under water. Alternatively, cover the stem ends with cooking foil. On the other hand the ends can quite easily be cut away if they do show signs of mould.

As I said earlier, one of the loveliest of preserved materials is wild clematis. I have given more details about this plant in the chapter on autumn, but here I want to say that sometimes it is possible also to preserve the foliage left on the seed stems. Some years this is easier than others, and I cannot really say why except that it appears to be a matter of growth. When the plant has ripened well in a good summer the leaves are tougher than usual and they then seem to take the solution more readily. I usually keep the foliage on in anticipation of success and then prune it away afterwards if it has failed to take.

It is a great pity that we cannot retain the lovely hues of some foliage by this method, but no matter how often I have tried and with whatever variations in method, I have never been able to get anything but a serviceable brown from branches of, say viburnum and hawthorn, which were beautifully red when I stood them in the solution. Some, like the sycamore, do not even turn brown, but usually drop their leaves, although here I must confess that I have not yet tried gathering these branches early in the year. I generally press sycamore instead as, indeed, I press many other leaves, from ferns to individual fallen leaves, especially of such lovely things as the aspen, with its silvery undersides, and the lance-shaped sweet chestnut.

There are various ways of pressing branches and individual leaves, the simplest being to lay them out between sheets of newspaper and put them under the carpet where people will walk over them frequently. Take care though that you do not do too much vacuum cleaning at this point or you may find leaf confetti instead! Individual leaves, which fit nicely between the absorbent pages of non-glossy magazines, can go under a chair cushion. You can also use marble slabs, large books and even a sprinkling of sand over newspaper. Leaves you have gathered individually and which seem already almost dry but slightly curled can be pressed with an iron.

Incidentally I have discovered a good way of keeping green ferns, such as the Male Fern, *Dryopteris filix-mas*, looking fresh and green for many weeks. The fronds must be mature, so glance on the underside and see that the brown spores are formed. Condition the fronds thoroughly and then stand them in the glycerine mixture for at least forty-eight hours. After this they can be arranged in plain water. If you want good green ferns after pressing, first give them this treatment and then press.

Bracken must be gathered before it has become completely

43

brown and it is best pressed. It is possible to preserve the fronds by steeping them in the glycerine solution, but this entails using a considerable amount, as you would expect, and the fronds must then be dried by pressing. Even then they are inclined to feel slightly sticky, and personally I prefer to press them fresh.

If you are of an experimental turn of mind I am sure you will enjoy treating many kinds of seeding stems with the glycerine preparation. You will have some unexpected colours as a result. You need to gather them while they are still green, and they should be well conditioned beforehand so that they are strong and firm.

If you want to save some grasses for winter arrangement it is important to remember that these are best when they are gathered early in the year. If you wait until autumn the grasses will be over-ripe, often untidy because their shapes were spoiled when they shed their seeds, and too dry and brittle.

I begin picking some of them as early as late May and go on through early summer as they come into bloom. Cut young, when the grass flowerhead is just coming from its sheath, you can capture much of their true colour, and it is surprising how many hues there are.

Pick the grasses and hang them, head downwards, in small bunches in some cool, shady place to dry. Once they are dry to the touch you can store them in boxes until you are ready to use them.

The same applies to the many pretty rushes which you can find in moist places, like the common *Juncus inflexus* or Hard Rush and the Soft Rush, *J. effusus*, which has a rounder head than the first. The sedges, too, can be treated like grasses, although in their case the inflorescences should be well grown but not mature.

Each year I receive a number of letters from readers asking how best to preserve the reed mace or bulrush. Sometimes they ask how they can stop the velvety heads from turning fluffy and disintegrating. It's the same old story: the stems are cut too mature. If the bulrushes are ripe, no matter how gently you handle them they will spill. This is, after all, how they have propagated themselves over millions of years, and the whims or desires of the casual flower arranger are of little import to them!

Gather these while they are still a lighter shade of brown than they will become when old. Wait until the male portion at the top of the inflorescence has withered and then cut the stems. Do not put them in water but stand them in some deep vessel to dry, preferably slowly in the normal atmosphere of the room.

Fungi can be dried in various ways. Tough fungi like the oyster bracket type can be dried simply by standing it on paper in a room. It will dry quicker if you place it in an airing cupboard, as will some of the other types.

Some of the more fleshy fungi can be dried in silica gel, a desiccant employed in many applications for removing moisture from the air. You can buy it from most chemist shops. It can be used time and time again. Use a covered box, cover the floor with the desiccant, place the fungus or fungi upon this, gills upwards, and shake the material over so that the fungi are completely buried.

It is not possible to say how long the fungi should be buried, for this will depend on size, moisture content, temperature, relative humidity and several other factors. Examine the contents of the box after twenty-four hours if the fungi are small, waiting a day or two longer if they are larger. Take them out when they feel completely dry to the touch and have obviously lost weight.

Sometimes you may be fortunate enough to find bracket fungi which have dried quite naturally on the tree, and these will need no further treatment.

In the woods you will often find lovely skeletonized or partly skeletonized leaves of all kinds, and it is well worth while searching the ground under trees for them. I remember how enchanted I was when I first discovered lace-like holly leaves. These look so pretty lightly touched with clear paint and glitter for Christmas decorations. Other skeletonized or shadow leaves are beautiful when arranged against the light. To arrange them you must mount them on false stems or branches and this is easily done with just a touch of colourless adhesive. You can use long grass straws for individual leaves and bare branches if you wish to create a branch. In this case it is interesting to try to match the leaf with a branch from its own tree.

If the leaves are stained and muddy you can wash them quite safely in detergent and then lay them out on newspaper to dry. You can make them lighter in hue by adding a little household bleach to the water in which they are washed.

In the early spring you can pick pussy willow to dry. It will keep quite well until the following winter, when you can use it in all kinds of arrangement of both dried and fresh materials. Simply cut it when it is grey and fluffy and well formed. Both the stems and the catkins will shrink a little after drying, so wait until they are nice and plump before gathering. Drying is simple: just stand them in an empty container or hang them upside-down in a cool, dry place.

I always like to dry a few alder catkins too, for these are great favourites of mine. I love the twisted, gnarled character of the branches. These make such interesting lines and shapes to frame a few fresh flowers or leaves gathered in mid winter. Like the pussy willow they are extremely long-lasting if you take care to handle them gently and to store them in such a way that they have no heavy materials resting on them.

Spring

As soon as the shortest day has passed one becomes aware that the buds on the willows are swelling and that the touch of grey silk on the pussy willow catkins is showing, already smudging the deeper, winter-coloured bark. Meanwhile the hazel catkins grow longer daily, except when snows and frost dominate the weather. On the alder they are just a gesture, but the female catkins, which do not mature until really late in the year, are still retained by the tree, hanging pendulous like little cones.

A few stems of hazel catkins will transform a bunch of daffodils from the shop, divesting them of their too perfect, uniform, greenhouse sophistication and giving them instead an air of the countryside and springtime in earnest.

Don't look for the finest branch on the bush. This is likely to be too stiff, too fan-shaped. See if, instead, you can find one which is imperfectly shaped, for this will simplify arrangement and give you a much more interesting line. If only perfectly shaped branches are available you may have to prune them. Remember to adjust the branch so that its tip comes over the centre of the base of the container. When you arrange the branches in a low trough and cut some of the lower stems away, place some at interesting angles so that they seem to be growing out from the centre to the front of the trough, encircling and protecting the flowers.

So many of the trees and shrubs will be changing colour, be it ever so slightly, but some are brilliant. If you have plain walls to your room try an arrangement of winter-red stems of dogwood, *Cornus sanguinea* or cornel, various willows and poplars. You may be lucky enough to find a lone, beautifully coloured bramble trail. Even in spring I have found these vividly scarlet. And in spring too one can sometimes find many berries. These look lovely with bare stems and newly opening leaves of forced branches.

In February the strange brick-red flowers of the elms brush the tall trees with a warm glow, bringing new and welcome colour to the countryside. These branches are curving and interesting to look at, splendid ploys for the adventurous in arrangement. Try them in line designs, as silhouettes featuring the flowering but leafless branches so that they repeat the theme of the winter landscape, shapes seen against winter skies.

There will be few other wildings to accompany the elm, but look out for ivy leaves growing on limestone walls. Often these redden beautifully and will harmonize with the elm blossoms. If you are buying flowers there are certain tulips and freesias which will harmonize beautifully, and, if you want something exotic and surprisingly long lasting, buy a spray of cymbidium orchids.

The earliest of our hedgerow blossom is the blackthorn, *Prunus spinosa*, the flower of the blue-black sloe (*see* Pl. III). The branches should be gathered when the buds are really no more than lightly coloured swellings on the stems. Many of the branches are nothing more than spiny thickets, so it is well worth searching the shrub for well-shaped stems. In any case branches will have to be pruned and shaped.

In some areas blackthorn branches are lichen covered and these are doubly decorative. Blossom always lasts much longer, surprisingly so sometimes, if you do not move the arrangement at all. Try to dust around it.

Blackthorn looks well in low dish arrangements. Try covering the dish with moss on the water and stud it like a miniature meadow with any tiny blooms you can find, even the lowest blossom clusters that were cut away from the stem end. If you are buying flowers, cut three narcissi short and place low at the foot of the blossom with a few large leaves among them.

From the end of March onwards we can expect to find catkins or blossom on all our wild trees, although few of these will be spectacularly coloured, for we have a preponderance of green, yellow and white. Even so, most are decorative in some way or another.

Catkins, as I stressed earlier, need to be gathered when young, and unless this is done they will not remain attractive for long after arrangement, for the warm, dry air that coaxes them to grow when they are young will hasten their life and cause them to shrivel once they are mature.

Late March and early April is the time when you can expect to find the birch ready to pick, the fine, pendulous branches thick with catkins and so pretty. Indoors the tiny, delicate leaves are bright green among the flowers. The branches are not easy to arrange, simply because they have to be set at such a different angle from the way they grow naturally. They are not so good as some others in low containers. I think that they are best lifted up, high from the table, in tall, slim vases a little like birch trunks, so that the stems can hang gracefully and the catkins naturally (Pl. IV). The oak catkins with their young foliage, often bronzed or looking like newly polished brass, make a particularly lovely combination, although some trees produce choicer materials than others and you might find it worth while to look around before cutting.

Many willows produce yellow catkins in April and May on their well-leaved stems. Poplars flower in April. The catkins of the black poplar, *Populus niger*, which likes wet woods, are tipped with russet. Those of the aspen, *P. tremula*, are downy grey, while the white poplar, *P. alba*, not really a native incidentally, are short and downy. Later in the year these leaves, which are snowy white beneath, are lovely with white flowers, and fallen leaves can be pressed and used for winter arrangements.

The 'Tassel tree' is our family name for the lovely sycamore, *Acer pseudoplatanus*, one of our two native trees of this genus, because of the delightful long pendant racemes of green-yellow flowers that hang from its branches in late spring and early summer. These flowering branches make heavenly decorations. One needs to prune away some of the leaves, but not too many, so that the tassels show to advantage. More important than pruning, I think, is the actual placement of stems. If a branch can be arranged almost at the horizontal, so that the flowers hang as they would on a tree, a very pleasing effect is obtained and enchanting arrangements can be made.

The field or hedge maple, *Acer campestre*, produces smaller racemes. As soon as the flowers have faded one should keep an eye on this dainty tree, for the winged fruits or keys which follow the tassels colour beautifully, corals and reds of many hues among the greens. Stems of these, pruned entirely of their leaves, can be used with fresh flowers. They cascade charmingly over the rims of vases, and thus may be used in much the same way as a bunch of grapes is used in a more lush decoration.

After they have served their purpose in fresh arrangements they can be stood or hung up to dry for use in perpetuelle arrangements. When dried they change colour to a soft biscuit tan, but it is hard to forecast exactly what their colour will be as this depends on season, humidity, length of drying period and other similar matters.

The nutmeg-fragrant blossoms of the hawthorn or may, *Crataegus monogyna*, follow the blackthorn. These are long lasting, but like other blossom they live longest if they can be picked and arranged while they are in bud (*see* Pl. 14). The branches are leafy as well as flowery. When they are being mixed with other flowers it is best to lessen their density by nipping off the leaf clusters that have no flowers close to the stem. This way you retain quite a lot of foliage and the flowers are not hidden by the surplus leaves. Beware of the spines!

If hawthorn was rare I am sure we would pay the earth for it, yet I have met many, many people who have never given it a second glance nor thought of using it as a cut flower. You can arrange it with choice flowers (white ones look especially lovely), carnations, tulips, freesias and roses as well as the simpler kinds. Consider it for decorations for a wedding.

Technically the horse chestnut, *Aesculus hippocastanum*, is not a wild plant. It is believed to have been introduced to Britain some time in the sixteenth century. Yet to many people who leave town to visit the country this tree must surely seem an essential part of the wayside. It seldom grows casually. It is mainly planted in farmlands, parklands, along roadsides and in gardens, yet we are lucky enough to have a few trees growing wild not far from our home as well as a couple of examples grown from seedlings in our own garden.

For years I wanted to arrange the handsome 'candles', but I always seemed to be too much engaged in something else at the time they appeared, until quite recently. I had noticed how the branches grow, outwards, tips downwards in spring and summer when they are laden, and curving upwards in winter, to become almost upright in early spring when their buds are swelling, each tip directed to the reluctant sun. This led me to believe that the stems might be pliable, and so they are. It is possible to coax them to assume many angles, which is just as well, for if you try to arrange the stems just as you pick them it is not possible to make a normal sized arrangement (*see* Pl. 12). The ideal would be to have a great bowl in some enormous room and to anchor one great branch in it, its angle as near as could be to the position it took on the tree. (*See* my notes on this in Chapter Four.)

Described as a troublesome weed, the pretty coltsfoot, *Tussilago farfara*, can be found growing almost anywhere in ordinary soils, quite often by the roadsides and on waste ground from early March. Knowing that it is so common, and that it is certain to propagate itself too quickly for many people, I lift the roots complete for arrangement. The flowers last much better this way, and if you lift them as the first flowers are opening you also get a pleasant succession of the yellow blooms. They look best in strong, sturdy pots, like brown casseroles. The flowers come before their leaves, which are large and handsomely shaped, with grey undersides. I like to use these in summer green arrangements.

Almost the first hedgerow plants to be taken are the wild arums. Their leaves are much like other foliage. If they are gathered young they will not take water well or easily. Later in the year they seem to become much more hardened, but in the early days of spring it is best to pull the whole group of leaves. This entire group, or alternatively individual leaves if these are cut, should be stood and hardened in tepid water.

The beautiful sagittate foliage is invaluable for arranging with bunches of bought flowers that do not have sufficient foliage of their own. All narcissi, for example, look lovely arranged in a low bowl on a pinholder with a flourish of leaves at the foot of the stems, these also hiding the holder incidentally. The foliage can also be used at rim level in a tall vase and will 'face' nicely, cutting its mass and linking it with the flowers it holds. By carefully unfolding the arum leaf cluster you can find individual leaves with really good, long stems.

Some weeks after the first leaves show the green arum lilies open. Coiled tightly and tidily at first, they end their days by flapping their spathes like pale green banners (*see* Pl. 1). But cut young and treated in the same way as you harden the leaves they

last well in water. They are delightful in green foliage arrangements. Later in the season the spathes disappear and the seeds
being fertilized swell inside a berry-like fruit, poisonous but
extremely handsome, growing thickly studded on fat stems (*see*
Pl. 4).

We can expect to find the irresistible little field daisies, *Bellis
perennis*, at any time during winter according to both locality and
weather. Obviously just a few of these tiny morsels are not greatly
decorative on their own, but for picture story arrangements the
entire plants can be used, a good way of weeding the lawn. Uproot
the plant and wash its roots under running water. If you use a
pinholder you can impale it by the crown quite easily. Alternatively use the ring method (*see* p. 26).

When gathering these daisies try to pick those which are the
youngest. Any that are in bud and just showing their pretty,
carmine-tipped petals are suitable. The general rules about fresh-
ness apply as much for these tiny flowers as for their larger and
cultivated cousins. Inspect the centre of the disc and note whether
the florets which form it are mature or young. If they are open and
polleny then they are too old and will not last long. On the other
hand, if you are gathering them only for a party decoration they
will live long enough.

As children, I remember, we used to sit in the meadow grass on
a spring morning with a bare or just breaking twig of hawthorn
chosen for its prickliness and a bunch of daisies which we would
behead and impale on the twig, each flower to a thorn. Then we
had a branch of blossom—our childish way, I imagine, to hurry
spring along!

Now that I am older this form of decoration does not appeal to
me so much, but I know that one can make charming though not
very long-lasting party decorations by using straws or long,
strong grasses or reeds and threading the daisies onto them. It is
best to choose a meadow grass such as timothy, which can be cut
short at the top and buried in the centre of the top daisy. Several
stems of these threaded daisies look attractive on a raised buffet
decoration, in a candle cup, for example.

For a party daisies can be strewn over the table top, just laid
apparently haphazard. Alternatively, circle the centre of the table
with daisy chains. To make these slit open the portion near the
base of the stem with a thumbnail and thread the stem of another
daisy through. Pierce the stem end of this, and so on until the

chain is long enough. Should you wish to save the flowers, simply unlink them and stand them in deep water.

Daisies are also rather charming made into small, tight little Victorian posies, with perhaps a wild rosebud in the centre, and laid on the table napkins as individual table decorations.

One way to use posies, each collared with ivy leaves, is to place them among ivy trails used to decorate the apron of a buffet table, charming for a wedding. Moon daisies can also be used in this way. The posies should not be too large or they then become difficult to arrange. Generally speaking a posy with the thickness of a daffodil stem is large enough.

For a simple and quick decoration for a dinner party or similar occasion, use candle cups holding white, pink or green candles to match the flowers, and surround them with a ring of daisy posies each with its own outer ring or collar of leaves. I like to use small pointed leaves—ivy is quite good and always plentiful—so that they resemble a ring of ray florets, rather like the daisy itself. In fact the arrangement follows the flower's design: it looks like a great daisy with a candle at the centre (*see* Pl. 10). Following this theme further, small dishes can be filled with rings of posies around the candle.

There are so many daisies other than the little field daisy that you can find throughout the year, and all look pretty arranged in styles like those just described.

Say 'daisies' and it is probable that another flower, the buttercup, will also spring to mind. How pretty these are! And how delightful they look with little daisies. And how charming the two when they have the blue germander speedwell, *Veronica chamaedrys*, arranged with them (*see* Pl. 19). There are few flowers which are so blue. This speedwell grows only too well in some gardens, mine included, but we have allowed it to settle down in the meadow area, where I can find it in flower from March to August. Its stems are longer and less stiff than the daisies, and so for small arrangements it can be arranged at the back and edges of a design (*see* Pl. VII).

There are many species of buttercups to arrange with the speedwell, flowering as late as September. All have one thing in common, the glorious sheen on the inside of the petals. I once saw two lady visitors to a flower club exhibition examining an arrangement of these little flowers and pondering aloud over whether or not the petals had been painted with nail varnish.

They certainly had not, but so bright were they that anyone could be forgiven for thinking that someone had varnished the lily. (*See* Pls. VI, VII, 22.)

Open buttercups do not last long, but those gathered in bud will stay lovely several days after opening in water. Treat short-stemmed flowers as you would daisies.

Few flowers are as welcome as the lesser celandine, *Ranunculus ficaria*, for once the first green-yellow buds are seen rising above the newly formed glossy leaves we can be certain that the other spring flowers will not be long in following. The little flowers are frail, as are many others that have soft, sappy stems.

This is one of the few wild plants I prefer to uproot, for they then last longer and are in my opinion more attractively arranged. They are ideal for picture story arrangements. The cut flowers can be posied. If you care to replant the roots in your garden you can provide for yourself a pretty little ground cover plant which is little trouble. I have several areas of it in my garden. The glossy green leaves which appear in early spring quickly become studded with flowers and together they smother the ground, yet there is little left of them by summer except the tiny tubers from which they are propagated. The flowers return each spring.

For someone who relies on wild flowers and weeds for decoration, the dead nettle family proves extremely useful. Almost as soon as the days begin imperceptibly to grow longer the pink dead nettle, *Lamium purpureum*, begins to flower. Usually the first that I see are in my vegetable patch, from which I have no compunction about uprooting them and bringing them indoors.

Sometimes, where the soil is very good, comparatively large plants can be found, and then individual stems can be picked. But usually the plant is bushy rather than tall. Like most of the fragile weeds this is a plant which is best pulled up by the roots and arranged whole. The little dead nettle soon settles down in water and arranges itself quite prettily. Growing in water the leaves sometimes change colour and so bring a little unexpected joy. Whole plants are ideal for placing at the foot of a branch.

Three or four plants will completely fill an average sized bowl for the table. And because it is so early in the year and flowers are scarce the little blooms always bring pleasure and receive praise. Whole roots can be used as a base or mat for other flowers, so arranged that they rise up from them. If you buy flowers, try pink lamium and blue grape hyacinths or small true hyacinths, snow-drops, or even the magenta blooms from a few bunches of mixed anemones arranged this way. Often the pale blue *Veronica persica*, the Persian speedwell, is blooming at the same time. Lamium and speedwell daisies, and the first celandines, make charming mixtures for low tables.

Later in the year the white dead nettle, *Lamium album*, is in flower, usually beginning somewhere about March, though much depends on the weather and the amount of protection the plant has found. It goes on and on and can be found plentiful again in autumn. (*See* Pls. VII, IX, 21.)

This is a handsome plant, but the white, beautifully formed labiate flowers are partly hidden by the leaves. I am not fond of defoliated flowers, but often it is necessary to remove a number of leaves in order to see the bloom. This must be done carefully, otherwise the flowers' fine shape will be marred by the ragged end of leaf left below them. Use a pair of pointed or grape scissors and cut the leaf right away with part of its tiny stem as well. The leaf can be pinched off but avoid stripping the outer skin from the main stem, for if this happens the stems will wilt and may not take water well.

Use the dead nettles as a filler for bowls for table decorations. They last a long time in water, and because of their distinctive shape, as well as the purity of the white flowers, they are good companions for flowers of all kinds in mixed arrangements.

In late spring when the bluebells begin to cover the woods and on into summer the yellow dead nettle or Yellow Archangel, *Galeobdolon luteum*, also blooms. This is, I think, one of the most attractive of our spring plants. It is quite long lasting and makes a bright and pleasant contrast to the bluebells and rose campion which are in bloom at the same time. The yellow dead nettle, like the white, is improved if some of its leaves are removed to reveal the flowers. The alternative to removing the leaves is to arrange the stems in a tall, slim vase so that one can look up to them and so see under the leaves where the flowers grow.

Use dead nettles with taller, branching subjects, arranging them so that they radiate from the base of some curving stem. Later their green seeding stems look well in foliage arrangements.

The familiar and much loved cow parsley, *Anthriscus sylvestris*, in flower from late April to June, actually gives decorative material throughout most of the year—all the year indeed if you consider the umbels of seeds for winter and Christmas decorations. (*See* Pls. IX, 13, 22, 23.)

In the early days of spring it is one of the first to thrust its leaves above the soil. These are then compact and ferny, fresh and a lovely green. They are very attractive and deserve to be used, but like so much other immature foliage they do not take water readily and easily. They must be properly hardened. Beware also that when they are arranged the leaves do not siphon water from the vase.

Once the plant is in bloom the stems are very long, and cow parsley can be used as a tall ingredient in any kind of arrangement. Try it with white flowers from the garden. Alternatively, short stems make lovely bowls and cones.

The umbels of seeds are attractive in their green state and so are useful throughout summer, especially in foliage arrangements. If they are to be used for winter arrangements the umbels should be gathered and dried before the seed is ripe or else it will fall and the umbels will be mere skeletons.

In sheltered parts of my garden the herb Robert, *Geranium robertianum*, one of the cranesbills, is among the first summer flowers to bloom, often in April (*see* Pls. 7, 13). The delightful thing about this plant, apart from its touchingly lovely little flowers, is that it is such a pretty plant as a whole. The finely cut leaves grow at first in a close, attractive rosette, which can be used entire. Where the soil is sparse and the sunlight good the leaves keep fairly small. I like to gather these individually and use them in early spring with all kinds of little flowers. They colour quite early in life and so are doubly useful. Sometimes they are as red as a pot geranium's petals.

Where the soil is good and there is also partial shade the plants reach a fine size and produce long and branching stems. In the woods near our country cottage in autumn the entire plants growing alongside a bridle path turn a brilliant colour as soon as they begin to seed. Stems and leaves alike become cerise.

Despite the fragile appearance of this little plant it lasts well in water, but like the other wild geraniums herb Robert is fleeting in its floral beauty. It compensates us in many ways, however, not least in the colour of the bills, which become more and more conspicuous after the petals have fallen.

This is another plant which is best uprooted and used whole. If the bowl is carefully chosen the leaves can flow over and hide the rim. Try an entire plant in a candle cup with other delicate little flowers gracefully rising up from the mat of leaves.

A whole plant is useful for masking or hiding a pinholder, especially in an arrangement where taller branches are used. Then I like to use more than one plant to furnish the space behind the branches as well as before them. When I do this I sometimes pick a few extra, longer-stemmed leaves and arrange them separately, so that they can continue the theme of the plant spreading throughout the decoration. The vividly coloured leaves thrown up at various times throughout the year will keep their colour when pressed. They are then very useful for flower pictures and plaques. If you buy flowers, use herb Robert with red anemones.

Often flowering in late autumn and sometimes throughout the winter in sheltered places, the primroses' real season is in April and May.

As children we used to go off on primrose-picking expeditions, a ball of soft wool in our pockets to tie the stems, and when we had picked a bunch and collared it with primrose leaves, we tied it with others onto a stripped elder cane. We carried these posy-studded poles home with great pride. There were more flowers, fewer people then. Nowadays I advise that, although the primroses, *Primula vulgaris*, are perennial and free-flowering, it is best to take a few blooms from each plant rather than rob one of all. (*See* Pls. III, IV, VII, 18.)

These flowers last well in water, yet although they are so soft in texture, that one might imagine it would improve them to be dunked, actually their blooms should not be allowed to go under water at all. Once they become immersed the petals lose their colour. Even if they are wet when gathered they should be well shaken to swish the surplus water from them.

Usually where there are primroses there are violets near by. There are several species of viola native to Britain, but the earliest of all is *Viola odorata*, which blooms even in February. The most frequent colours are white, purple and violet, although in some parts of the country one can find red violets. Like commercially grown violets, the wild flowers will quickly dry and die in the artificial atmosphere of the home. They can be made to last longer if they are given greater humidity. A little posy of wild violets is best sunk up to its neck in moist gravel, sand or moss. Alternatively, one can use a block or cylinder of Oasis and make a hole in the centre for the flowers' stems. You can also arrange the flowers inside a large brandy balloon or some similar glass, where they will live for much longer than in the drier air of the open room.

To make this more attractive one can create a tiny garden or country scene inside the glass, using a branch of elm flower, hazel or willow to form a little tree.

Small posies of violets collared with their own leaves may be laid in a circle on wet moss around a candle for a table centre. These flowers look delightful as a natural '*petit point*' massed in posies with other tiny flowers on moss in a deep meat dish or similar shallow bowl.

seven

Summer

I wonder why almost all of our native shrubs and trees should have blossom which is either white or some hue of green? Not for us the redbuds, the bougainvillea, the jacarandas. It is perhaps just as well that flower arrangers generally look particularly kindly on all-white arrangements.

To me summer begins when the creamy corymbs of elder flowers lace the bushes (*see* Pls. X, 20). Country people used to tell me that once the elder bloomed we could expect no more frosts, and as a child I believed them and, uncharacteristically, have gone on believing. Elder, *Sambucus niger*, does not grow so large or so plentifully as it did then, which is a pity, for apart from the elder-berry wine which so many people made from the berries, the birds feed from them too. However, where they do grow they are usually abundant, and the long, slender, cane-like stems studded with large, flat corymbs or clusters of flowers or berries can be used most effectively for quite large and certainly glamorous decorations.

Like many another soft-leaved plant, elder will not take water well if all the foliage is left on the blossoming stems, so a number of leaves should be cut away. I like to do this after the stems have been placed in position, so that the way I prune adds emphasis to a certain line, or alternatively serves to accentuate the creaminess of the blossom.

When branches are being gathered it is as well to keep an eye open for those which are badly shaped on the bush. On regularly trimmed hedges or shrubs the canes usually grow tall and erect, and although these are eminently suitable for the back or intermediate positions in an arrangement they are not so attractive at other angles. For nicely flowing stems to flow gracefully over the rim of a container, especially where really large decorations are planned, and for nicely angled stems for oriental type arrangements, bent or curved stems are most helpful to the arranger.

Elder stems are quite malleable, especially shortly after their ends have been stood in warm water. It is possible gently to press a flower stem so that its angle to the main stem is slightly changed and the blossom better displayed.

Personally I find the perfume of the elder flower slightly unpleasant, and so when I have to use it I often try to group some other very strongly scented flowers with it. I once used elder as a foil for pale blue delphiniums and apricot and orange lilies which dominated everything else with their own perfume.

Elder flower does not travel well if it has been stood in water. When it is necessary to transport it cut the branches, allow plenty of leaves to remain on to help protect the flowers and pack dry in bags as recommended in Chapter Four on caring for flowers.

Incidentally the young hollow stems can be used to raise those flowers such as begonias which have no good long stem of their own. Simply cut them to suitable lengths, fill them with water and arrange the short flower stem in the top of the hollow. Hollow stems of many plants can be used this way.

Breaking the rule about the white or green blossom, the wild roses have mainly pink-flowered species. There are a surprising number, the most common being the dog rose, *Rosa canina*, which is a soft shell pink. Rare in the south, but frequently seen farther north, the northern downy rose, R. *sherardii*, is much deeper in hue. It has round fruits with long, persistent calyces unlike the hips or heps of the dog rose, which are bare. Also a lover of the north, where it is common, is R. *villosa*, the soft-leaved rose, a dainty, deep pink flower. On calcareous soils you may be lucky enough to find R. *rubiginosa*, the sweet briar, so named because its foliage is scented. There is a lesser sweet briar, R. *micrantha*, very much more like the dog rose, and it too loses its sepals from the tips of the fruits.

There are still more, enough to make it worth while to devote some time to a summer search. I have left my favourite until last. It is R. *arvensis*, the trailing rose, with an attractive purple-tinged stem, white flowers and little round fruits. It is common here in the south-west. It is most often to be found growing in shade in June and July, and I have found stray flowers even late in the summer.

The only way to enjoy wild flowers is to cut them in bud. The calyx should just be opening back from the petals. If you cut them after they have opened they may drop their petals by the time you reach home. They last very much longer if you treat them like garden roses and add a little of Gregory's Rose Nutrient to the water.

Broom, *Sarothamnus scoparius*, is a great favourite with skilled flower arrangers, and they look on it with more favour when it is green than when it is in bloom. For this reason I have included it in the chapter on winter arrangements. This pretty shrub is a plant of the heathlands, common and widely distributed. Its performance in arrangements can be disappointing. This is when the flowers are too mature at the time of gathering. It should be collected when in bud with the lowest flowers on the stem only just ready to open.

Although by now I should be so familiar with it, every summer finds me surprised not only to see once again just how common is the common honeysuckle, *Lonicera periclymenum*, but also how delicately beautiful it is and how charming its character. Its custard-creamy flowers embellish miles of hedgerows, festoon hundreds of woodland trees and scent the air wherever it grows. It flowers from June to September and its blooms are followed by clusters of shining berries.

But this again can be a disappointment to the flower arranger, and once more its failure to live as prettily in a vase as it did on its vine is due to mature flowers, not buds, being gathered. If you want honeysuckle to look well and to last, and the clusters to remain entire, gather only those stems which bear unopened blooms and harden these well before arrangement. (*See* Pl. VIII.)

Belonging to the same tribe, though not the same family as the honeysuckle, are two of our loveliest native shrubs, the wayfaring tree, *Viburnum lantana* and the guelder rose, *V. opulus*, the latter being the species which gave rise to that fascinating garden tree, *V. opulus sterile*, the snowball tree, so called after the white pompon blooms, although I prefer the local name of Whitsuntide bosses.

The first is common to all but acid soils. It was one of the first shrubs I ever knew by name, my education on the subject of wild flowers coming via Messrs W. D. & H. O. Wills's cigarette cards. I remember that at the time I was given the card the flat corymbs of fruit on the bushes everywhere were green and red with some black among them. It was a revelation to me to recognize in life what was illustrated on the tobacco-scented card.

This shrub has a much stiffer habit than the guelder rose. It opens early in the year. Indeed, I like to gather it in late March and April when the young opening buds of blossom are mealy and their shape and habit strangely beautiful.

V. opulus prefers woods and grows also in damp hedgerows, which explains why it likes the border near the well in our garden, an area where the soil is always moist. The flowers are very handsome, creamy-white, with tiny florets at the centre, ringed by a circle of large, sterile florets.

This is one of the few shrubs which force well. Gather it, if you must, in bud and watch it open in water. It is not an easy subject to arrange, like the garden forms. The laterals are opposite each other, a type of growth which presents difficulties to the flower arranger. To get them to fall and flow attractively stems have to be carefully pruned and arranged with care, thought and attention.

It is pleasant to reflect that many plants growing in gardens are there because their owners fell in love with them growing wild. This is the reason why we have planted a lime, *Tilia*, in our plot. We chose the common lime, *T.* × *europea*, which is not really a native. Perhaps, since we are on limestone, we should have chosen *T. cordata*, the small-leaved lime, which you find in woods or growing on limestone cliffs. In any case the flowers, which bloom in July, are fragrant and beautifully made, an arranger's delight.

Lime needs a lot of grooming if it is to be effective when arranged. Unless the foliage, or almost all of it, is cut away the blossom branches will never become sufficiently turgid. Later, when the flowers fade and are replaced by winged fruits, the branches are still attractive. This is the time to preserve them in glycerine, and this time some of the leaves can be retained if you wish.

I lost my heart to the soft pink blossom of the bramble *Rubus ulmifolium* long ago, and in spite of my prejudice against using plants with thorny stems never a year passes without I make some arrangements of the sweet pink flowers (how the bees love them!)

and their luscious looking fruits, so beautifully made. Most flowers have bright yellow centres, which I like, but this bramble has not. Instead the stamens are soft dove grey. The undersides of the leaves are silver grey also and they prompt the arranger to search for other silvers to arrange with them.

I find that it is best to gather the stems with flower-gatherers, which unlike other secateurs will cut and hold the stem as one brings it from the plant. Since so many grow almost out of reach this is important.

To ensure that the stems take water quickly and can be arranged easily I find that it is best immediately to scrape the stem ends free from thorns. This entails removing a little of the outer bark by scraping the stem with a knife or using rose de-thorning tongs. This way it is possible to handle the stems easily, otherwise the thorns from one stem tend to get entangled with those from another and they are then most exasperating.

Bramble blossom buds continue to open in water. Stems of blackberries are extremely long lasting when arranged. Green berries ripen. I like to use the stems of these fruits with garden flowers and I have more to say about them in the chapter on autumn.

Later in the season the foliage of many species of rubus become beautifully coloured. A lone, vivid branch is sufficient to inspire one to create lovely autumnal colour harmonies. Unlike many other coloured leaves at this season the bramble will continue to take water and will last well. Only occasionally can one find a bramble shoot which has both coloured foliage and fruit clusters. Usually, when arrangements featuring mainly brambles are assembled, one must search for the coloured foliage and with them arrange the separate stems on which green, red and black berries vie with each other in producing the prettiest show.

I think it was Charles Darwin who said that this might be one of the plants we were watching actually in the process of evolution, changing from a deciduous plant into an evergreen. Certainly from autumn and on through the winter one can gather fine stems to bring a new shape and a useful touch of summer green to decorations. The vines are grand for wall vases and for pedestal arrangements. They look lovely in mid-winter arranged with arching stems of rose hips and fragile seed umbels of cow parsley and others.

At the end of August onwards you can expect to find odd

branches of vividly coloured leaves even though autumn itself is still some time away. I recollect that even while the rest of the tree is still deep green an occasional branch of the hawthorn will be seen to be the most vivid rose-red and yellow, and attractively shaped oak branches are chrome with green veins. In fact at this season some leaves are often a much brighter colour than they are when the true fall comes.

Among the most beautiful of all our wild materials, in my opinion, are the grasses, which are legion. They can be used both fresh and dried, but as you would expect they are loveliest when fresh. I enjoy gathering a bunch of mixed grasses as much as I do anything else, and arranging them is, for me, a real relaxation because this is something you just cannot hurry. Although I use them mainly with other flowers, at times I make a large arrangement from nothing but mixed grasses. An arrangement of this kind has one advantage over others, for if I wish I can simply leave it to dry. This can be a real exercise in arrangement.

In arrangements of fresh mixed flowers I find the meadow cat's tail or timothy grass, *Phleum pratense*, both useful and attractive; useful in giving height and line, and attractive for its green spikes, some three to four inches in length. It is in flower from mid May until August. There is a smaller species, *P. bertolonii*, the lesser cat's tail, which you can find growing on grassy hills.

I am sure that most people will have their own favourites as far as grasses are concerned, just as they do with all other flowers. As you would expect, some are much more decorative than others. (*See* Pls. VI, X, 18, 23, 27.)

It is impossible to go for a walk outside a town without finding some kind or other of grass. I do not intend to list them all. Just remember that they should be gathered on the mature side. To watch them mature in water is a delight. When they grow naturally we seldom have an opportunity to observe them so closely.

There are several handsome grasses in woods and in hedgerows. The perennial woodland brome, *Bromus ramosus*, is a wonderful grass for arrangers who are looking for something which is both very tall, two to four feet, and strikingly graceful. Fortunately for me this grass is plentiful along the lane which leads to our cottage, but as it grows up through the actual hedge it is often difficult to pick it without damaging it, and I have to pull it through with great care, stem end first.

I have made some very effective Christmas arrangements from this brome. The pendulous, inch-long spikelets which form the grass head look lovely when lightly painted and glittered. The stems are so long and strong that the grasses can be made into a giant fountain-like arrangement.

The quaking grasses, *Briza media* and *B. minor*, are great favourites. The first is common on limy soils. Many people grow them as garden plants and harvest the grasses for winter decorations. We used to call them wigwams, and I remember seeing vases full of them in so many cottage windows, where they were displayed with pride.

They also prompt me to think of moon daisies! I have so many happy childhood memories of walking through the long meadow grass gathering wigwams, sorrel, moon-daisies and sometimes orchids in fields long since gone.

The tiny field daisy becomes less plentiful as the summer comes. It is early replaced by the moon or ox-eye daisy, *Chrysanthemum leucanthemum*, which goes on flowering until August. Thriving and flowering most generously in poor soil it can be found almost everywhere.

Most flower arrangements will become enhanced by a knot of gleaming white daisies as their hearts. You might like to do as I often do and use moon daisies with a mixture of bought pink and red pyrethrums. These flowers are so similar in appearance, and if you pick with discrimination, selecting only the largest moon daisies, there will not be much difference in size between the wild and cultivated ones. You can then fill a vase or bowl full of vari-coloured daisies, which looks extremely attractive.

If you need some companions you will find that all the daisies will look well with grasses and other cereals. The moon daisy itself is as long lasting as most bought chrysanthemums and so can form the basis of many home arrangements such as table decorations. Do take care to strip the foliage from the stem ends before starting the arrangement.

One effective way of displaying them is to use the theme of daisies in the grass. Preserved barley or even fresh green wild barley and brome, with red poppy anemones if you can find no actual poppies, will make a charming party theme. You may be lucky enough also to have a few bright blue cornflowers, and then you will be able to make a really fresh and gay decoration. Wicker or straw containers look well with these flowers, just as a straw hat does or used to do when garlands were worn around the crown.

More summer daisies are to be found in both yellow and white. The chamomiles are charming. There are several species. The sweet-scented kind (it goes under two names: *Chamaemelum nobile* and *Anthemis nobilis*) grows on sandy soil. It is a sprawling plant, and although charming is really not quite so useful for flower arrangement as its less aromatic cousin, the stinking chamomile, which really has a libellous name. It flowers only through June and July while the other, *Anthemis cotula*, flowers from July to September. Another, the corn chamomile, *A. arvensis*, which is slightly sweetly scented, flowers also in June and July only. This one has fairly large daisy heads, about an inch in diameter, but it is not quite so free-flowering as *A. cotula*.

Actually I have found that in certain seasons one can gather this species as late as November, and as I do not find its perfume offensive I gather it quite freely. One year I had a bonus when we bought a little extra ground at the end of our garden. To our surprise, for we had never seen the plant so prolific in this plot before, the ground was covered with this anthemis, growing along with oats and peppermints.

In autumn it is worth looking for a late root of anthemis to arrange with a mixture of red, black and green berries. They really are extremely effective and they last so much better on root.

They make a pleasant link between mixed flowers and white pottery when this is used to hold them. As I have white walls everywhere in my country cottage I favour a knot of white flowers, particularly daisies, in mixed arrangements because the decoration then becomes 'nailed' to the wall rather than set apart from it.

When individual stems are arranged these, like most branching flowers, need some cutting or pruning to get the best from them. Although a stem of chamomile might appear to have flowers growing all at one level, it can be cut in such a way that one is left with a tall stem with a few flowers and some shorter lengths to arrange lower down or to mass at and below rim level.

Also with scented leaves (they remind me of the garden tagetes) is *Chrysanthemum parthenium*, the feverfew or batchelor's buttons, flowering in July and August in both cultivated soil and waste places. I have found it growing in walls. This is a really good flower for cutting. Stems grow from eighteen inches to two feet in height.

Often seen in gardens, mainly in its double form, *Achillea ptarmica*, or sneezewort, is common in wet meadows and on moors. The individual daisies in the clusters on the long stems are not quite so well defined as the feverfew, their centre discs not being so yellow, but it is a 'good arranger' just the same. It looks well with grey-green leaves and grasses.

The sea aster, *Aster tripolium*, blooms from July to September in salt marshes where it is common, looking for all the world like a garden Michaelmas daisy at first glance. Fleabane, or *Pulicaria dysentiarica*, grows in wet meadows or in ditches, its flat, golden yellow heads distinctive among its tribe. The stems grow to two feet. The leaves are woolly, which indicates to us that the flower must be well hardened before use.

I like to use the yellow ragworts, which look especially well, I think, with those end-of-summer, harvest festival type of decorations one makes with blackberries, bracken, autumnal-tinted leaves and clematis. They belong to the groundsel or senecio family. Oxford ragwort, *Senecio squalidus* (what a name to give a flower!) has spread its way from Oxford, where it was local before the advent of steam, along the railways, and is now locally abundant in many places. Another ragwort, growing taller and blooming much later, until October, can be found growing on old pastures which are not cultivated as they should be. Be sure to harden these properly.

On waysides and in waste places, including those by the sea, you may find one or other of the artemesias. *A. vulgaris*, or mugwort, and *A. maritima*, which is much more downy or woolly, are both aromatic and can be used in pot-pourris. Gathered before the flowers are mature, the flowering stems dry well and can be used in perpetuelle arrangements.

Not all members of the compositae tribe resemble daisies. Take the purple-pink hemp agrimony, *Eupatorium cannabinum*, for example. You would have to look carefully to see that the soft, feathery bloom is composed of many tiny rayless florets.

I remember with amusement the story once told me by Mary Pope, one of the pioneers of flower clubs in this country, of how, when she and a friend journeyed to London to lecture to members and friends of the Delphinium Society on decorations with delphiniums, they stopped on the way to gather armfuls of this handsome flower growing so profusely in the ditches by the roadside. The reason they chose this particular plant was because in colour and shape it was such a wonderful contrast to the tall delphinium spikes.

You can find hemp agrimony growing almost anywhere in ditches and stream sides or in moist ground near by, flowering from July to September. Its tall, three-foot stems will take water well so long as they have been well hardened.

Also common in certain areas, but where the soil is dry this time, is golden rod, *Solidago virgaurea*. It is a much less spectacular plant than the golden rod of gardens, which are hybrids of American species. But even so its golden, daisy-studded stems are quite pretty.

Also among the compositae are the teasels and thistles, but I have included these in the chapter on autumn flowers.

No one is likely to grumble at you if you gather poppies by the armful, but you might grumble at yourself when you reach home to find nothing but a bunch of limp, petal-dropping blooms. Poppies are delightful flowers for arrangement, but they need gathering wisely. Pick only buds, particularly those which are plump and obviously petal-full. As soon as you have picked enough, tap the bunch to make the stem ends level and take a match or cigarette lighter and hold it to the base of the stems and singe them well. This will prevent the poppies from bleeding and will also ensure that they will take water properly. On reaching home place the singed stems immediately in deep tepid water for at least an hour before arrangement proper.

The poppy seedboxes or capsules are also useful to the decorator. At the end of summer look for the round capsules of *Papaver rhoeas*, for these make little grape-shaped bunches for inclusion in Christmas decorations. Hang the seed stems in small bunches to dry. The stems become nicely wiry and will not snap when bound together.

P. dubium and *P. argemone*, the long, rough-headed poppy, both have long capsules which look well in mixed arrangements of other dried flowers. Shake out the seeds before bringing the capsules home.

The delightful red or rose campion, *Silene dioica* (*see* Pl. VIII), jostles the bluebells in the woods and all the other flowers in the hedgerows where it loves to grow, opening shyly and slowly at first until all the countryside blushes for its exuberance. I have always loved this flower, perhaps because although its season is said to be summer, actually blooms can be seen for months afterwards. I have admired it at Christmas, shining rosily above the frosted grass.

Plants of rose campion that appear uninvited in my garden are usually given border room. Because they do not have the crowded wild plants around them, which in spite of competing for survival actually also help to support them, the plants often have to be given a surround of twiggy sticks like many other of my garden perennials. Both flowers and foliage are soft and sappy and so wilt quickly. They should be cut in bud if possible and be well hardened. This being done they will last well.

Enthusiasts for 'wooden' arrangements should go in search of the seeding stems. The green calyces develop into attractive pitcher-like capsules on tall, branching stems.

The papery clusters of the inflated calyces of the bladder campion, *Silene vulgaris*, have a quaint charm. Their slender stems hang gracefully, and the soft grey-green of them harmonizes so prettily with many other plants. A plant of both pastures and waste places, this campion looks very attractive arranged with grasses among which you can find it growing in fields. On waste land you may find the plant spread out, covering a surprising area. Once I had a plant appear on my roof garden in the centre of London's Covent Garden market, and there it prettily graced a portion of my low peat-brick wall for a surprisingly long period.

Silene alba, the white campion, flowers from May to September. Its thick white petals and clean-cut shape appeal to me, and I use it quite often in all-white arrangements, even among garden plants. But then, why not? Plants of *S. alba* grow in the border. The seed pods are decorative, both when green and when ripe.

Not far from where the drift of rose campion is allowed to grow in our garden there are also various vetches, and quite recently I was enchanted to find another member of their tribe, Papilionaceae, the bird's-foot trefoil. There it was, spreading out on the short grass, smothered with the charming clusters of bright yellow flowers, their buds tinged with orange, a welcome visitor, but one on which we will have to keep an eye just the same.

As a child I was enchanted to learn that the little flowers we knew as Tom Thumbs were in fact *Lotus corniculatus*. Having been told the poem we children imagined ourselves lotus-eaters as we sucked the honey from the tiny flowers.

This is a beautiful little plant, common everywhere, continuing in flower from June to September. Actually the flowers are too short-stemmed for easy arrangement. I wonder now at the patience one had as a child, when one sat among the meadow grass and carefully assembled a posy to take home. But these posies arranged in a simple beaker are often far lovelier than any more self-conscious arrangement.

Another pretty way to display these blooms is roughly as they grow. Use a low container. Cut some of the leafy growths and arrange these below the mass of flowers, letting the trails, some with flowers still attached, flow well away from the rim of the bowl.

A species with larger flowers is the marsh bird's-foot trefoil, which is common in wet meadows and boggy places. Other trefoils are trifolium and not lotus, and while some are very modest little flowers not suitable for flower arrangement others are extremely handsome. Take the rosy clovers, for instance, the abundant *T. pratense*, the red clover, which grows in pastures everywhere from May to early autumn and has handsome tripartite leaves with a silvery white central zone, and *T. medium*, the zigzag clover which grows mostly on clay soils beginning to flower a month later, with larger flowers than the first and a deeper colour, veering to red-purple.

Very handsome but not a true native is *T. incarnatum*, the crimson clover, really a fodder crop, although it makes itself very much at home on some roadsides. To me it is a joy to behold. The flower heads are longer and more tightly packed than the other clovers. When the florets fade an attractive grey-green seed head remains. What a find for a flower arranger this is! Sweetly scented and full of honey, the blooms covering square yards of ground, is the Dutch or white clover, *T. repens*, which goes on blooming until October.

These clovers all last well in water, and since their leaves are so handsome they are distinctive enough to stand on their own, although they also look well in mixed arrangements. I love to mix them with daisies (*see* Pl. II).

I like to look around any area where I find them growing before I begin to pick the flowers because some are much longer stemmed than others. The white clovers vary too, obviously according to the richness of the soil on which they are growing. Sometimes the heads are really large and the stems long. Like the bird's-foot trefoil these white clovers look attractive arranged much as they grow. You can find trailing pieces of leafy stems on the plants. They can also be posied, all white or red and white together and used in ways suggested for daisies and other tiny flowers. The longer stemmed red and zigzag clovers look very pretty arranged with meadow grasses. You are certain to find some growing near by.

In this same 'butterfly-flowered' tribe, Papilionaceae, we have the pretty vetches and the closely related sainfoin, *Onobrychis viciifolia*, a truly lovely plant with handsome pyramidal flower spikes of a clear pink borne on erect stems, some one to two feet high. This again is a farmer's crop, for the plants are rich in nitrogen, although it is native on chalk. Its leaves are long and pinnate, fine for all-foliage arrangements. You can buy seeds of sainfoin and it deserves a place in any flower garden. It is long lasting in water.

In hedgerows and fields you are certain to see the yellow vetchling, *Lathyrus pratensis*, where it flowers from June to September. The flower stalks are fairly long and they can be picked separately like the garden sweet pea to which it is so nearly related. If you want longer stems these too, like the tufted vetch, need cutting carefully if they are not to break or bend. The long pods are delightful in all-green arrangements.

During June until August in hedgerows, and sometimes in thickets or weaving its way through a great mass of bramble, the showy tufted vetch, *Vicia cracca*, flaunts its long, curving spikes of violet-coloured flowers. Given the right conditions the climbing vines will reach as high as six feet, clasping tightly with frail tendrils borne on the end of graceful pinnate leaves, which are often fine and silky.

The stems need gathering very carefully, for in spite of their seeming toughness in being able to claw through the most forbidding spiny thickets they are actually fragile. There is often danger of one damaging the whole plant in trying to take just a stem or two. You need to take time and exercise patience to sort out one from the rest before cutting each properly with flower-gatherers or secateurs.

I love the long, mimosa-like leaves, each ladder or feather terminating in a contorted tendril. Stems of this foliage give a pretty flourish to small arrangements, and they need not necessarily include the vetch blooms themselves, for they are just as attractive though of a different colour value when they bear the little pods.

Indeed, the foliage of many other vetches is useful in this respect and can play an important part in all-foliage arrangements as well (*see* Pls. II, VII, VIII, 19).

Vetch pods are fun, first green, then various tans, browns and even black. The hairy tare, a common weed and with an unremarkable flower, has little black pods useful for tiny dried arrangements.

The bush vetch, *V. sepium*, is a decorative little flower. It is not so elegant, but its leaves are fuller and larger. I let it grow in a few places in our garden. *V. sativa*, which often naturalizes itself in cultivated ground, also appears there. Its foliage too is more distinctive than its flowers, which though pretty are too sparse to be useful.

In June and July great masses of white and yellow bedstraw can be seen covering the ground, often on waysides. *Galium verum*, lady's bedstraw, is yellow and is common in dry places. *G. mollugo*, hedge bedstraw, is white and also common. You will see it trailing in and out and foaming from the foot of hedgerows, often on three- to four-foot stems.

Bedstraws are frothy, fluffy flowers full of the scent of summer. They are extremely long lasting when cut, but the stems need to be gathered carefully. Don't try to take a great handful by tearing indiscriminately at the plant; instead, if you exercise a little patience to disentangle the branches you will be able to select just the number you need of long, tapering stems, which will look so attractive at the edges of a flower arrangement. Once the flowers have faded there remains a pretty green seed head structure. This too, as might be expected, is useful for decorations and looks particularly lovely where all green or all foliage arrangements are being assembled. These stems can be dried, but they will not keep the particular bright apple green they are when they are fresh. Even so, they still have good decorative value.

Fumaria officinalis, a dainty little plant, is a weed of fields and gardens. It is so very charming that I always have difficulty in bringing myself to uproot it when I find it in my borders. I compromise by allowing it to remain in one area, around the base of an apple tree, where it covers the circle of soil with its fine delicate leaves and long spikes of purple-pink tubular flowers. I use the entire plant in summer arrangements. Soft and sappy, the cut individual stems do not always take water well and it is best to arrange it on root.

The entire plant is prettily formed, and you will find that a large specimen or two or more can be easily supported by stones in a low bowl, where they will look very attractive. Fumitory arranged this way forms a good basis for other flowers, especially those that have leafless stems, sweet peas, for example. I particularly like pansies with fumitory. There are many other fumitories, but none really suitable for flower arrangement.

The geraniums or cranesbills, on the other hand, are really worth getting to know. In some areas the purple-blue flowers of the meadow cranesbill colours roadsides as well as fields and banks all summer through. What lovely things they are! No wonder some species and varieties feature so much in so many gardens.

These flowers are often fleeting in their beauty once they are picked. The petals drop as easily from them as they do from their cultivated cousins, the more sophisticated pot geraniums, really pelargoniums. If the precise pattern of the flower arrangement does not concern you, so that if on one day a flower to the left is in bloom and on another there is one on the right, then you will enjoy the ever-opening buds and revel in the little seedbox left bare by the falling petals. It is this which gives the flower its homely name of cranesbill.

Actually the petals can be fixed for a while by applying a spot of floral gum or gum arabic, or even a little colourless nail varnish, if you have the patience to apply it at the base of each petal. Use a manicure orange stick to do this.

However, as pretty as the flowers are, I recommend more their leaves. All through summer in all species you will find many that are most splendidly coloured—vivid reds, yellows and orange. Those which are just changing hue last longest. Those which are highly coloured will not always take water, for after all they are being discarded by the plant and their biological processes are changing, but they will certainly last a few days.

They may also be pressed, on stem, and later used in both fresh and dried arrangements, but I should warn you that the lovely red hues are not always retained after pressing. More often the leaves turn a brown tinted with yellow. Fortunately the stem remains strong. I use these quite a lot in arrangements made from dried helichrysums and other garden flowers. The leaves from the smaller species are useful for flower pictures. The green leaves will take water well enough, and these attractively shaped, rough-textured forms look well in all-foliage arrangements.

Another much smaller-flowered geranium, *G. lucidum*, the shining cranesbill, which grows on acid soils, has another type of foliage to offer: bright apple green, glossy and very lovely. Its flowers are small and insignificant, but in spite of this its stems are decorative and graceful. Like the herb Robert they are dainty enough to be used with all other kinds of flowers. The red stems are attractive. This tiny geranium is common on acid soils where it grows mainly in the shade, flowering from May to August.

Plants of the umbelliferae seem always to be with us. Even while the first leaves are showing, the empty, fluted stems of last year's crop stand skeletal above them, the ribs of the umbels reminding one of the flowers they bore then. There are a great many species, some appearing only locally, some rare, some common. Most are white, with attractive green seeding umbels. Some species are extremely dainty, *Pimpinella saxifraga*, for example, which you will find growing among grass except on acid soils, and its larger cousin *P. major*, which grows along roadsides as well as in fields.

The wild angelica, *A. sylvestris*, flowering through summer until September, has pink and white flowers clustered in a fairly loose umbel. It is common in damp meadows and some roadsides where the soil is moist. Occasionally you can find the garden angelica, *A. archangelica* or *A. officinalis*, growing in damp meadows or along river banks. Its umbels are almost globular and green, handsome focal points for certain arrangements.

Wild parsnip, *Peucedanum sativum*, has yellow flowers and grows on limy soils. Its hollow stem is deeply furrowed, and when I arrange it I like to feature the stems, using cut portions to fan out to the side of the flowers. These I arrange vertically, smallest at the tip, largest umbel (perhaps one that is seeding) at the base. This is an easy to do, effective pattern for all stiff-stemmed flowers.

Flowering in July and August and sometimes into September, and common in hedgerows, is the hedge parsley, *Torilis japonica*, which I think is one of the most graceful of all the umbelliferae. Its dainty flowers bring a touch of lace to arrangements of the more robust rose heps and other berries and in late summer autumnal foliage. Probably because it blooms later in the year the hedge parsley is longer lasting than the cow parsley of spring and early summer. The small umbels, carefully flattened, press well and are pretty used in real flower pictures.

Although it does not have the grace of some others of this tribe, the cow parsnip or hogweed, *Heracleum sphondylium*, so common everywhere, has many uses for the flower arranger (*see* Pl. 26). Often in early summer when it is first in bloom it is passed over in favour of other flowers, but later in the year the white umbels are still in flower. I have gathered them as late as the last week in November. These look very attractive in mixed arrangements when berries are used. But they also look well on their own arranged in a low dish in such a way that one flat umbel rises above the other towards a young opening bloom at the tip.

It is always rewarding to search among the plants for foliage that has become well coloured. Cow parsnip and cow parsley foliage often turns a beautiful yellow or even a pale ivory and sometimes a dark plum purple. Such leaves are long lasting in water provided they were not actually dying when they were gathered. If they appear to be limp on the plant they will press well and can be used for pictures, when the fronds and small portions of the leaves will be found useful and attractive. The fully mature umbels can be hung up in a cool, shady, airy place and dried for winter arrangements, as can most of this tribe of umbelliferae.

Often in summer the kerbside vendors in Covent Garden market have as part of their stock bundles of long, tail-like, greenery-yallery flowers of the dyer's greenweed, *Reseda luteola*, which they grandly call 'wild mignonette'. Certainly it is from the same family as that sweet-scented plant, which also grows wild on chalky soil, but the greenweed has neither its scent nor its colour.

There are three wild mignonettes, R. *alba*, R. *lutea* and R. *luteola*, flowering from June to August. The first can be found in waste places. The other two you are almost certain to see from your car window as you drive through chalky and limestone country, for they seem to love the roadsides.

Like all green flowers there are times when they are extremely useful to the flower arranger. I have friends who grow the greenweed in the garden because of its value in this respect. All the plants are also highly decorative in their seed-bearing stage. The spicate shapes provide interesting contrast to all kinds of rounded forms without dominating them. They are ideal for all green flower arrangements.

The golden charlock, *Sinapsis arvensis*, and the white mustard, S. *alba*, both abundant on farmland and often covering the verges of newly built roads where their oily seeds, long dormant in the soil, have been brought to the surface by the bulldozers, flower brilliantly in early summer. In the same family, cruciferae, is the sweetly perfumed dame's violet, *Hesperis matronalis*, really an alien. You may find this tall crucifer, white or lilac, growing by a riverside, often in large drifts, and strongly scenting the air.

Closely related to the garden honesty is the penny cress, *Thlaspi arvense*, whose flowers more resemble the humble shepherd's purse than the showy garden plant. Its decorative value lies in its almost round, large, flat seed pods, half to three-quarters of an inch long and reminiscent of those of honesty except that they are both winged and notched. The stems carrying the seed pods are often a foot or even more in height. They are useful and pretty for green arrangements. Gathered young and hung upside-down to dry they become biscuit-coloured and look attractive in dried arrangements.

Covering hillsides, carpeting acres of ground, filling woodland clearings and beautifying waste and burnt ground, the rose bay, *Chamaenerion angustifolium*, is surely one of our most lovely plants. We can gather it without guilt. It propagates itself freely—one might almost say eagerly. Its long, graceful stems are useful in flower decoration. Being spicate they contrast prettily with all kinds of rounded shapes, flowers, foliage or fruits. The purple-pink hue of the blooms and the darker tones in stems and seed pods harmonize beautifully with coloured autumn fruits.

But it is another of those plants that do not take kindly to water immediately. Stem ends sometimes have to be cut more than once or the flowers will wilt and not take up water quickly enough. The main cause of wilting is that the flowers are too mature when cut. Quite a large portion of the spike should be in bloom before the stems will take water readily. Hot water treatment, of course, is always effective.

The seed pods of this rose bay willowherb are most attractive and are coloured like the flowers. They can be used for dried arrangements, but in this case one has to take care that they are cut when they are young because should they be too mature they will continue to develop in water, and one morning you will discover that your flower arrangement is a great mass of fluffy, cottonwool-like seed styles. If you like this effect treat with hair spray to anchor the 'cotton'.

In one bed in our garden, mingling with mainly white and lavender flowers, we have plants that have grey and downy or silver foliage. These are both shrubby and herbaceous, and among the latter the common mullein, *Verbascum thapsus*, is the most distinctive, holding its own with and indeed far superior to many of the more 'choice' imported plants.

The leaves and stem are covered with a soft, silvery down. The long, aspiring stem is studded with pretty, five-petalled yellow flowers in July and August. Mullein is common on dry soils and you will often see it in considerable numbers on some roadsides.

Like those of most silver plants, leaves of mullein can be pressed and later mounted on false stems and used in dried arrangements. If you gather them for this purpose select the most perfect and lay them flat one on the other for transport and press them singly as soon as you get home.

Although *Potentilla anserina*, the feathery silverweed, blooms in high summer, its charming little flowers are really not so important to the flower arranger as its leaves. You will find it carpeting waste ground, roadsides, or among grasses in moist pastures. I know a place on the edge of a wood where it borders the bridle path and so delightfully does it clothe the ground beneath the wild shrubs there that I go several times a year to admire it. It is stoloniferous, so I once filched a few runners and planted them in our silver border. Here the plant is so satisfied with its cool, shady position between santolina and anaphalis and under senecio that it produces wonderful silver 'feathers' some six or seven inches long.

The little yellow cinquefoil blooms have all the charm of the potentillas, but are really not showy or plentiful enough to make them useful to the decorator. Gather the leaves when they are mature and they will take water well. I use them with all kinds of flowers, and their long, graceful pinnate shape gives pleasant contrast to so many things. They press well and are especially beautiful in flower pictures and montage arrangements.

The handsome hop, much more common than many people realize, climbs through hedgerows in July and August, twisting and weaving green ropes of vine-like leaves tasselled with tiny, fragile male flowers and handsome bracted cones of female flowers which later form the attractive bunches of hops used for brewing. These are delightful components in flower arrangements. Cut the stems carefully so that bunches can be easily arranged to flow pendant over the container rims.

If you want to arrange some of the stems so that they stand

high, be guided by the plant's natural growth, use some tall, slender but firm stem and help the vine to climb it. Usually it is a simple matter to hook the hop stem in the axils of leaf stems retained by the support. Failing this use a little discreet Sellotape here and there.

In the garden one of the prettiest and most effective ground covers is the variegated bugle, *Ajuga reptans variegata*. The wild species with plain green leaves, but the same pretty blue labiate flower, is quite common and grows prolifically in damp ground. From May to July it makes a deep violet-blue pattern among the grass. The stems are not very long, so the flower is confined mainly to low arrangements. I like to use it as a backcloth to cow parsley, filling a low bowl with the bugle and then arranging the cow parsley stems among it.

Nearly related to it is wood sage, *Teucrium scorodonia*, with spikes of yellow-green flowers growing on foot-high stems clothed with alternate pairs of culinary sage-like leaves. Here is a plant you can use in all-green arrangements. As you would expect, it grows in woods and is easily found, for it is quite common.

The common persicaria, *Polygonum persicaria*, its long, soft leaves handsomely coloured with dark wine-red blotches, bears long, slender stems of little spikes of pink flower, looking like clusters of embroiderer's French knots. The plant appears as a garden weed and is also common on damp ground in the wild. The flowers have a long season, from June to September. It is not a flower for individual arrangement, but it is useful in mixtures, especially where the stems can be arranged at the extremities, as, for example, in a small pedestal arrangement.

The docks and sorrel, rumex, are wild relatives of the garden rhubarb, and species of both contribute attractive ingredients to many flower arrangements which can be either fresh or dried.

The broad-leaved dock, R. *obtusifolius*, can be very beautiful, the young flowering stems green tinged with ruby. It grows in hedges and along the margins of fields. Also common, its leaves and flowers a slightly darker green, is the curled dock, R. *crispus*, its long, spear-shaped foliage having curled margins. These docks flower from July onwards.

The common sorrel, R. *aceta*, often grows among the grasses in pastures, bringing a warm russet hue to the scene. This flowers earlier than the dock, usually in late May.

The inflorescences of these plants are in the form of a long, graceful spike. First of all, so far as the dock is concerned, this is a bright green, later turning colour. The sorrel is a rusty red from the beginning. Both can be dried so long as they are gathered in good time. If the flowers are mature and the seeds already forming then they will drop badly, so they must be gathered while they are still of good colour and still young. They can then be hung upside-down in the usual way in a cool shady place until they are dry.

On certain soils and under certain conditions the leaves will turn a most delightful rhubarb red, much more decorative than the usual somewhat drab dock green. One way of making the plants colour is to pull them up by the roots and throw the plant down in moist grass, or alternatively leave them in a plastic bag. In either case inspect the plants to make sure that they do not harbour slugs, snails or any other pests.

Pennywort, *Umbilicus rupestris*, is a fascinating little green flower, a spire of bells rising from round, lobed leaves, which give the plant its name. It grows from crevices in rocks and walls, and although it prefers acid soils, where it is common, I first made its acquaintance at Englishcombe near Bath, which is on limestone. Green and succulent when fresh, it also dries well, even naturally, for you can return to a colony of pennywort in late autumn and gather stems to last the winter.

eight

Autumn

From late summer onwards, sometimes into midwinter, the berry clusters on the long vines of black bryony, *Tamus communis*, weaving through the hedgerows, become more conspicuous than they were when they bore the tiny heart-shaped leaves. First a glossy green, later a showy, vivid mixture of green, yellow, orange and red, these very poisonous berries must really be among the handsomest fruits we have growing wild (*see* Pls. XI, XII).

I have used them ever since I can remember, not only because I admire their decorative qualities, especially when the berries are multicoloured and still unripe, but also because they last a long time in water. They can also be used out of water, and even then they are still long lived.

The vines wind around each other as they grow, often making thick ropes. It is possible to unwind these and to use the long individual curving trails of clustered fruits and yellowing leaves. As you would imagine, these are best reserved for special decorations such as swags for Hallowe'en. More practically, it is best to divide the vines into convenient portions, cutting them through directly above a berry cluster so that this terminates the portion of stem below.

Incidentally, if you find some bryony but do not wish to use it until some days ahead, cut the vines, disarranging them as little as possible, and store them by placing them in a large polythene bag.

Close it and lay it on the ground outdoors in some place out of the sun.

Many times I have used bryony clusters as focal points in arrangements of winter evergreens, carrying the berry colour from the base, up through the arrangement to the tip. The largest clusters are set low while any small groups, even twos or threes, are saved for the tips or extremities of the arrangement.

In tall arrangements it is often necessary to mount the cut sections on false stems of some kind. Quite the simplest method is to use an 18-gauge florist wire and insert this up the stem as far as it will penetrate. Once used, wires can be cut and used again. If the berry cluster is very heavy one wire will not always hold it in place, so in this case insert two or more wires together. Alternatively, use a fine stem—privet and willow wands are excellent for this purpose—and lash the bryony stem to it with adhesive tape, raffia or twine. If you use the tape see that all surfaces are quite dry or it may not hold securely.

Although the bryony leaves turn a pleasant chrome and yellow hue they do not live long once the stem has been cut. You would find them suitable for arrangements of a one-day-stand nature but not for any longer-lived plans you may have unless the leaves are only just beginning to change hue.

On calcareous soils in the south the wild *Clematis vitalba* (old man's beard) is a feature of the countryside. The long vines weave among the hedge plants, festoon tall trees and furnish walls. I have always been happy that I have lived in clematis country because I find the creamy green flowers and their feathery seed-heads a perennial joy (*see* Pls. XII, XIV).

The plant begins to bloom in July. The flowering stems are borne in opposite pairs on the strong, rope-like vines. Cut short, these flowering stems are both useful and attractive for low arrangements. One favourite mixture of mine is clematis and purple vetch or sometimes the purple everlasting pea from my cottage wall. They look lovely also with sweet peas and with dahlias.

Like many of the buttercup family clematis can be temperamental. The ease with which water is taken up depends a great deal upon the maturity of the flowers, the season, the weather and, I have no doubt, other unknown factors. So to be on the safe side always harden both the long trails and the short flower stems by standing the ends in boiling water. As with bryony, a long stem can be cut into sections of a more convenient length.

Stems which bear pairs of opposite stems or laterals, of which the *Viburnum opulus* is another example, are often difficult to arrange in average-sized decorations. In fact these 'twins' are sometimes a great nuisance. It is always easier to arrange a single flower than a pair, for you will find that no matter how much you try to influence them they will persist in going in opposite directions, so I usually trim them. The piece cut away can be used in smaller decorations. (Fortunately the flower stems of clematis leave their main stems at a good angle, which means that where this is desired they can be arranged to flow out nicely and without much effort on the part of the arranger.)

Sometimes a portion of stem bearing two opposite flower stems can be treated to make the two seem like one flower spike. As a rule all that is necessary is to twist one around the other, even crooking two inside one of the usually twisted leaf stems, or alternatively to hook one into the other.

The actual flowering season of this clematis spreads over a long period, and it is quite usual to find a few blossoms on a vine which is already producing the fluffy 'beards'.

Trailing stems are lovely, and elegant beyond words. Like so many wild species the stems of clematis have about them an air of timelessness and lack of period which is the hallmark of classic beauty. They look as much in harmony with garden lilies as they do with wild grasses.

Some people remove all the foliage from the stems in order to give greater prominence to the flowers. I used to do this myself, but I found that the denuded stems appealed to me less and less. Much depends upon the style of the arrangement, of course, but generally I allow as many leaves as possible or as is practical to remain on the stems. However, *all* damaged and insect-eaten foliage is removed, and if in taking one leaf I should disturb the pattern of the compound leaves I usually remove the whole section rather than allow it to remain incomplete.

As sweet as the flowers of clematis are, I think that they are surpassed in beauty by the whorled clusters of newly formed, feathery fruits. When young these are greenish, but the actual seeds, achenes, are reddish brown and these give an emphasis to the rest of the cluster. If these newly feathered stems are cut and arranged without any kind of preparation they quickly become fluffy and somewhat shapeless, and lose their fresh look. However, it is possible to delay the change by using a solution of glycerine and hot water as described in Chapter Five on preservation.

This also fixes the style and prevents the seed clusters from becoming disintegrated. If you arrange the old man's beard without its first being 'fixed' this way you will find that after a day or two the feathery styles will blow about the room and become a nuisance. Preserved, the clusters will last all winter through and even longer should this be necessary. I have even washed dusty heads in detergent by swishing them around in the lather and drying them by laying them on newspaper.

They must be given glycerine while they are young and fresh. You cannot fix the seed heads this way once they have become fluffy on the plant.

Although the leaves of clematis are soft they will also some-times take the glycerine solution and turn a deep bronze in colour. I have tried pressing any which have been especially attractively coloured, but I have always found that the compound leaves separate.

Trails of feathered clematis can play many roles in autumnal and winter arrangements, and the pleasing thing is that once you have preserved them you can use them time and time again. As you would expect they look lovely with all kinds of bought flowers, especially chrysanthemums. They harmonize most prettily with berry mixtures and with all kinds of autumn tinted foliage.

Some trails are very long indeed. Incidentally, look in the grass at the foot of a vine, for you will often find very long stems grow-ing along the ground, and these are much easier to pick. The way you divide these trails into portions can simplify arrangement con-siderably. Set aside tapering tips to act as upright stems and to place at the edges of an arrangement, and divide the remainder of the stem into portions, each tipped with a good flower stem.

Seed stems, which do not have to reach water, can be lengthened in the same manner as recommended for bryony.

If you find the long trails of either flowers or seeding stems too supple to stand upright, try stiffening the lower stem portion by wiring it with a long 20-gauge wire. Bind it in widely spaced spirals. Begin at the base and hold the stem upside-down as you wire it. This done, insert it in the vase and exert gentle pressure on the wired portion until the tip falls into the required position.

Most people, and not least flower arrangers, appreciate the glowing, shiny fruits, the heps or hips of the several wild roses, and look forward to their season. Fortunately they are not hard to find and you might as well take any you find in the hedgerows, for they are almost certain to be trimmed before summer comes again (*see* Pls. 30–31, 33).

Usually the hips turn colour before the leaves have dropped, and for a time the bush is very colourful. The foliage of the pale pink dog rose is never very flamboyant, but it is attractive just the same. If the leaves are only just turning colour you can make some pretty arrangements of foliage and fruit, but if the colouring process is fairly well advanced the leaves will fall quite quickly once the stems are cut. The smaller leaves of R. *arvensis* and the fern-like foliage of R. *pimpinellifolia* are longer lasting.

You can often find the hips glowing throughout winter, some-times even into early spring, though perhaps then you will think as I do, that spring-evoking catkins and young leaves, rather than autumn's symbols, are more welcome in the home. Like most fruits they look well with many kinds of flowers, but try using them with their own race. Mix them with bought roses. They look surprisingly attractive together, obviously because there is this blood- or should we say sap-relationship between the two. Although you might expect some incongruity in a marriage of such ultra-sophistication and wildings, actually one enhances the other pleasantly.

Where your roses are short-stemmed the long arching wild briars can help you define bold and perhaps unusual lines and also decorate a wide area should this be necessary. I have in mind an arrangement I often make in a tall, slim but heavy modern ceramic vase from which the berried stems stretch out, each well displayed, arching out yet protecting the few roses which lean out, massed close together in a knot of scented colour over the rim.

You will find that a framework of rose hips arranged in a low container will serve you well for many weeks during the winter months, and you can sit many a little bought flower at their feet. Ring the changes with anemones, individual blooms cut from spray chrysanthemums and vivid nerines. If you have no blooms use foliage instead, even a few dark green leaves of laurel will look good, especially if you arrange a vivid cluster of more hips before them so that each colour beautifully complements the other.

I like to use the slender lateral stems, each terminated by a cluster of hips, in a bowl for a table centre. I first arrange a base of shorter stems of some foliage, box, for instance, and then arrange the rose stems to rise from this. Often I recess larger flowers a little below the berry clusters. Anemones are usually my choice here, especially as the scarlet ones in a bunch can be chosen for this purpose and the mauve and purple ones reserved for some other kind of berries, bramble or privet, for example.

The important thing is to select those stems which are well endowed with fruits to act as the main lines in arrangements and to pick extra shorter laterals to provide a fuller colour mass where this is required.

The thorns will have to be removed from the lower parts of the stems if you are to arrange the stems both quickly and easily. Personally I find this best to do when I am actually gathering the stems. If you wear gloves you will find that after a little practice you can quickly snap the thorns off by bending them away from the stem with the flat of your thumb. Otherwise scrape them off with a knife, making a downwards movement, or use the simple tong-like strippers freely available now. Once the stem ends are thornless you will find the bunch much easier to hold and to slip into a bag. Take care that the thorns on the remainder of the stem don't tear the plastic.

I like to gather a good bunch of some of the smaller laterals besides taking some of the longer stems. Hips can be used for many decorations other than actual flower arrangement. They are pretty used in party pieces. At Christmas they can be used with all the seasonal evergreens, and personally I see no objection to using them with holly if all you have in the garden or can find in the woods is what we call 'blind' or berry-less.

When we were children we always talked of 'hips and haws'. In our minds they were as closely associated as cat and dog or eggs and bacon! I imagine they must have been paired this way for centuries uncounted, possibly because they ripen together. We used to pick them, of course, but we also nibbled them, carefully avoiding the seeds in the hips because these have tiny, spiny hairs which tickle your throat and keep you coughing for hours should you swallow one or more.

The haws are the fruits of the may tree or hawthorn. The berries themselves are in attractive clusters and are of a dark crimson colour, but the heavily loaded branched are often difficult to arrange. This is because they are often angular as well as heavy.

What I find best to do is to select a good branch with plenty of bright berries, then to take time to arrange it, pulling it slowly from one side to another until it sits comfortably and looks at ease. From this point it can be pruned and the trimmings either set lower down at the stem base or used in some other arrangement. Like the rose hips, hawthorns too will harmonize with other flowers, but I like them best with the last of autumn's wild blooms, coloured foliage, grasses, cereals and other berries. The dark crimson is a good hue to have present in mixtures, for it provides a pleasant link between one contrasting colour and another.

The leaves often turn beautiful colours, but unfortunately I have never been able to retain any of these, although I have pressed the branches successfully from time to time. The only trouble is that the thorns often get in the way and make this a slightly difficult operation. One has to use a really heavy press, like a slab of marble, to keep the stems quite flat while the leaves are being pressed. Another method is to place the branches between thick sheets of newspaper after taping them to one piece to keep them in place and then put the newspaper under a carpet which is subjected to considerable use. Incidentally do not vacuum clean over it or you may find shredded paper and leaves instead of neatly pressed sheets.

Remember what I wrote earlier about lichened branches, and search particularly for hawthorn branches shrouded in this way. They can be very beautiful indeed and they look very lovely with the little exotics from the florist such as freesias, the first narcissi which now reach us from October onwards, chincherinchees and others with leafless stems and sculpted outlines to their blooms (*see* Pls. 15–17).

Black berries of all kinds strike me as being particularly handsome. They share with the more splendid grape an opulence that they seem to be able to shed on any other plant material you care to arrange with them no matter how simple. I suppose that this is due to the fact that the 'black' is really a deep shade of purple, a royal colour and one which is to be found in some greater or lesser degree in a surprising number of plant materials from buds, blooms, stems, stipules, undersides of leaves and so many other parts as well as fruits of all kinds.

For years now I have found great satisfaction in arranging the black berries of the privet, which turn colour in autumn and persist on the plant often until February. They grow in pyramidal clusters, reminiscent in some ways of an upright bunch of grapes, often on good, long, straight stems. However, these are seldom unbranched, having laterals often also terminated with a berry cluster, which needs to be trimmed to facilitate arrangement.

Like all other small stems these can be used in smaller decorations. I like to use them in conical arrangements which can be built up on a block of soaked Oasis which has been firmly wedged on a pedestal vase or a large goblet. If the vessel is kept filled with water the stem holder remains consistently moist. Cones of this nature look attractive when made of a variety of materials. First the surface should be covered by inserting very short snippets of box or some other dainty evergreen. The privet berries should be arranged in this in such a way that they protrude a little beyond the level of the foliage. They can be interspersed with some plant material such as other berries or tiny heads of flowering umbelliferae. The latter can look extremely attractive, like lace among black pearls.

If you plan to make a cone of any type of materials, first roughly grade the ingredients so that the largest can go around the cone in the first ring and work upwards from large to small. At the base insert the short stem ends so that they point upwards, and vary the angle so that by the time the middle section is reached they are being inserted horizontally, and above this they point slightly downwards until, at the very tip, the stems go down vertically.

Privet berries are fairly long lasting. Some long stems are nicely stiff and so can be used at the back of an arrangement, but also on a bush you can usually find well-shaped large clusters on arching stems which are just the thing for low-lying stems.

I like to make an arrangement of these black fruits in a black vase and then embroider it with a colour, ragwort or late feverfew daisies, for instance, or little dahlias from the garden or vivid pelargoniums from the window box picked because a frost is imminent, or even anemones from the flower-seller. These are particularly harmonious because of their blue-black centres.

Blackberries, bramble fruits are also great favourites of mine, and since they are good enough to eat (which is more than we can say for all the decorative berries!) as well as looking so, I like to use these as table decorations. They last surprisingly well. I have a few favourite containers for them: a pewter fruit dish, a green Wedgwood comport and a heavy glass bowl, which is the colour of blackberries crushed in cream. Like most other berries metal suits them very well, and they give one the opportunity of using vessels such as copper jelly-moulds, skillets, saucepans and tankards.

Sometimes I arrange them alone, but more often with some other flower or flowers, usually mixtures. They look fine with purple knapweed, rose bay, marjoram, late achillea and any late wild flower. They are simply superb with small dahlias, especially the mauve and rosy mauve pompon varieties.

As I said earlier, the spines on the stems can be a nuisance sometimes because through these one stem hooks onto another. The leaves sometimes behave in the same way. So I always shave the lower portions of stem with a sharp knife. Although the fruiting stem might look absolutely lovely when you see it growing, more than likely you will notice that it needs grooming when you take a closer look. I am continually surprised at the number of infertile fruits that need cutting away. This really is a worthwhile operation, for a groomed stem is so much more colourful and gleaming than one on which little bits of shabby materials remain.

Elderberries match a few pieces of glass I have, and so I am prompted annually to gather a few clusters and try out a new pattern with them. The heavy berried stems are not so easy to arrange as some, and the arranger has to do a little bit of gauging and assessing as well as coaxing to get them to hang prettily. I find that it is always necessary to spend a little longer than usual on the early stages of assembly when I am arranging long stems of elderberries. It is possible sometimes to twist a branch in such a way that when it is anchored the berry clusters are spread out like an open umbrella.

Short portions offer few problems beyond needing a little grooming or trimming. The flat clusters look well massed at rim level in a tall, narrow container with a few tall stems of some other subject behind them. I like to use the single stems of golden garden privet this way. The tall stems offer a pleasant contrast in shape to the berries and the colours harmonize, for in autumn the privet begins to take on new hues among which you can find the same purple as the berries (*see* Pls XV, 26, 28).

I like them also to form the deeply toned mass at low levels in arrangements with graceful trails of the fluffy old man's beard above and among them, and pale chrome yellow leaves behind them for colour and contrast. They look beautiful with rose bay, in whose tall spicate stems you can find hues to match the elder's fruits.

These are best gathered while some of them are still green, for then they last much longer, neither dropping nor shrivelling. And also at that time the birds will not have started on them so that they will not be damaged.

When you have finished with the berries in the arrangement tie them in a bunch and hang them out for the birds, even town sparrows. They will be much appreciated and, eventually, widely distributed.

The foliage of the elder may not be so useful as that of other shrubs during the year, but often in autumn it turns the most wonderful colours, varying from palest chrome through ruby and purple, harmonizing beautifully with the heavy corymbs of the purple-black shining berries. The hues seem to vary a good deal according both to the soil on which the bush is growing and the season. Sometimes the leaves turn a pallid hue and are not of great decorative consequence unless you are searching for very light tints. Yet even then this foliage is not as useful as you might think, for these very pale leaves are never of great substance and do not last as well as the greater purpled leaves.

Long branches are too large for average size decorations, but the handsome compound leaves can be used individually and are effective low in mixed arrangements or to frame groups of flowers, fruits and even vegetables. If when you make arrangements of this kind you include some elderberries you will establish a link with the foliage and other components which is very pleasing. It is possible to spread out the berries so that they lie flat over some underlying colour. Try them over very pale leaves.

Where you have seen the hedgerow white with blackthorn blossom in early spring, there you will find the grape-blue sloes, studding the angular thorned branches. They are long lasting in water, although as they mature the first blue changes slowly to a near black.

These are not easy branches to arrange. In the first place the ripened wood is stiff and unyielding and in the second fruiting branches have to be patiently groomed and bare stems and spines cut away if they are to give of their best. However, this is a chore I feel is well worth while. No other wild fruit has the colour or the texture of these little plums with the soft and lovely bloom on their skins. Try not to handle them or smudge them with leaves, so that you keep the bloom perfect. Arrange them with definite colours that will complement and prettily contrast the blue and give it greater value.

One of the loveliest decorations you can make is of mixed fruits and berries with the blue of the sloes, the crimson, reds, yellows and bright greens of the others, all definite colours, medieval in their simple opulence. To get the greatest effect mass some of the shorter branches together low in an arrangement.

No one could write about our beautiful wild plants without mentioning the spindle, *Euonymus europaeus*, whose coral, four-lobed fruits dangle daintily and profusely from thin, tough stems. This is such a beautiful shrub, its foliage turning vivid hues in autumn, that I cannot understand why more gardeners on seeing the plant growing wild do not rush out to buy one for themselves. There are some beautiful cultivars available, all either perfect plants for the small garden or to grow in groups in larger and more informal places.

The fruits open to disclose a bright orange aril which protects the seeds, and thus the spindle shows us a natural colour harmony which many say should never be attempted, that of sugar pink and orange. My advice is to pay no heed to dogmatic rules about colour. If you seek exciting adventures in colour, follow nature's example.

Although the branches of spindle berries are so lovely to look at they are not really easy to arrange, and sometimes, especially in mixed arrangements, the results can be most unsatisfactory. Spindle wood is skewer wood and was chosen originally not only because it is tough but also because it is straight. Side branches grow at stiff right angles to their main stems and so all need to be carefully cut, pruned and trimmed for arrangement if the result is not to be a tangled, meaningless mass.

You might find it best not to try to mix spindle with other plants, but instead to gather just one good stem (be sure to use secateurs or you will tear the bark and damage the plant). Give it a container to itself and let it stand as naturally as possible, a little stiff perhaps, but with its individual beauty on full display.

Woody nightshade, *Solanum dulcamara*, weaves its way through and scrambles along hedgerows or up through trees in copses or on the edges of some woods. From June to August it is covered with nodding clusters of dainty purple flowers like miniature potato blossoms. From these form the tiny, tomato-like berries and all summer long on one deep-green-leaved plant you can see all the stages and colours of maturity until finally, when the leaves fall, there are on the naked stems only the water-bright berries inviting the birds to come and feast.

Try arranging them in a white vase against a white wall. You will have to exercise a little patience as you work because stems belonging to a climbing plant are not stiff and sturdy and tend to move around. They often have to be embraced with arms of wire-netting at rim level here and there before they will stand just as you want them.

If the pendent nature of the flowers and fruits appeals as much to you as they do to me, you might like to follow a pattern of assembly I use for them. Select a tall, cylindrical vase. In its neck fit a mass of wire-netting, the cut ends protruding well above the rim. Pull the netting up at the back of the container near the rim so that it forms an inch or two of support to keep upright any stem arranged against it.

Break the general rules about sketching in the outline of the arrangement by using the tallest stems first, and begin instead by arranging stems in the foreground. Select the most pendulous stems for this area. When you insert the first stem see that it reaches water, but remember that its base does not necessarily have to go way down to the bottom of the vase—an inch under water will do. Let its lowest berry cluster reach down as low as you like, but see that it doesn't actually rest on the container. Pull it away a little if it tends to do this. You will find this quite easy to do if you wrap the wire ends around it at rim level and then push these upwards and outwards until the berries hang just as you want them. Arrange the next stem so that its terminal cluster falls a little above the lowest, to the left or right of it, and the next one to go a little higher than this and on the opposite side.

Now concentrate on finding a tall stem to go right at the very back. Fix this in position against the wire. Next fill in the spaces between the tip and the lowest cluster, selecting those stems which seem to fall in the right manner for the situations you wish to fill. You should be able to make some lovely lines this way. Cut away any surplus foliage as assembly proceeds. Mass berries and flowers on short stems at rim level, recessing some to give a greater depth of colour.

The gorgeous, glossy red berries of *Viburnum opulus*, the guelder rose, should be used with caution because once gathered and arranged they give off an unpleasant odour if they are kept too long. Use them fresh by all means, especially for decorations of short duration such as a harvest festival, but keep your nose on the alert!

On the other hand the foliage is dependable. Search the bush for odd branches and laterals. Young wood is too straight and, besides, it will produce next year's blossom. Look close to the main stems and fairly low on the bush, for it is there you are likely to find the best pieces. Once the foliage has completely turned colour it will not remain intact for long after cutting, but that which is just turning will continue to colour in water. Guelder rose foliage will not take a glycerine solution successfully.

From late September the hedge sycamore, *Acer campestre*, begins to change and become a wonderful tawny gold. Unfortunately these branches do not always take water as they should. The best way to preserve them for winter decoration is to press them. Even so, be selective and choose those which are as flat as possible or growing on one plane rather than branching in all directions. Those which are twiggy can be pruned a little so that only flat-growing portions remain. You can press the trimmings and give them false stems later when they are arranged,

These branches should then be spread out quite flat between sheets of newspaper and pressed under a carpet or some place where there will be a weight on them. The longer they can be left the better. The newspaper will extract any moisture from the leaves. They can then be taken out and used, dry and matt. If you have the patience it is a good idea to brush the leaves lightly with a little olive oil, not too much or they will become dusty and horrid, but the lightest smear will give them a little sheen which looks very natural. Some people varnish dried leaves, and you can buy varnish sprays. But this is really a matter of taste and patience.

Foliage of the common oak, *Quercus robur*, preserves well and is worth gathering for this purpose. Cut the branches immediately it is apparent that the leaves are changing colour and while the veins are still bright green. These will turn colour, but are likely to be a dark hue and not the natural oak gold of autumn. On the other hand, in late summer you will often find branches of prematurely coloured leaves lying below the tree. If these have only recently fallen they can be given the glycerine treatment. Judge by the look of the veins. If these are still green you will probably be successful. Alternatively such branches will often dry well, and branches which are not too thick and bulky can be pressed.

If you want acorns it is best to cut the branches while the nuts are still green and firmly fixed in their cups. They should then be given glycerine solution. Acorns picked up from beneath trees are inclined to shrink from the walls of the cup and fall out. If complete acorns are needed for decoration there is nothing for it but to sit patiently and fix each acorn by applying a little adhesive to its base before returning it to its cup.

Although hazel leaves cannot be persuaded to take the glycerine and water solution, it is possible to use this method to fix the little nut clusters on the stems. These will then turn brown. Gather the branches bearing nuts while they and their husks are still green. The nuts should be soft, with the kernel immature. Stand the branches in the solution and later prune away the shrivelled leaves. Later you can arrange them out of water by themselves or in pleasant mixtures with grasses and seed heads.

Beech mast can be preserved in the same way, although in this case the leaves will be retained. After preservation the four-valved cups open wide and resemble starry wooden flowers with silken linings. Sometimes the little cluster of triangular nuts are held in the centre of the 'flower', and these look very attractive.

If you are looking for something unusual for a special occasion, don't overlook the fruits of both the horse and the sweet chestnut. Before these are ripe they have beautiful green cases, very spiny in the case of the sweet nut and not quite so prickly for the conker cases. The particular hue of green, sharp and clear, looks well with purples and black, and the form and texture of the fruits are unusual enough to offer you a limitless choice of accompanying material.

Study the branches well before either cutting or arranging them. Those of the horse chestnut are likely to be more wayward. In either case you will need to prune away some of the foliage and rearrange it. Don't forget that the horse chestnut can be coaxed into shape if you want to alter the line a little.

Early in the season you can gather branches that bear a cluster of chestnuts still encased in their prickly shells. Arranged in water the cases open to reveal the gleaming brown nut inside. Later in the year, nearer ripening time, the cases will split and show the glossy mahogany brown nut inside. Clusters of these are extremely effective used as focal points in mixed arrangements.

The conkers which fall from the horse chestnut tree and strew the ground below from late September onwards are extremely beautiful yet seldom used in decorations. Like most fruits they become dry after a time, but while their glossy brown skins are at their best they can be used effectively. To keep them plump and shiny for as long as possible rub each nut with olive oil.

Conkers need to be mounted before they can be used. For a Grinling Gibbons type of 'wooden' swag, the nuts can be mounted by inserting a florist's wire in under the skin and bringing it out again about a half-inch farther on. The two ends of the wire can then be brought together and twisted once around each other close under the nut and finally brought down together as a double leg. You can impale the chestnuts on cocktail sticks, which can then be pushed into the top of a strong hollow straw for arrangement.

The purple knapweed, *Centaurea nigra*, is a little disappointing when cut because, like the sweet sultan of the garden, it does not remain so fluffy afterwards as when it is growing on the plant. Cut young flowers just emerging from the bud, not open blooms that might already be pollinated and so will not last.

The late blooms last better than any you might gather during the hot, dry days of summer. They look well with black and purple berries of all kinds. The stems are very tough and you will need pocket pruners or a knife to gather them.

When the flowers are finished, like most compositae they leave behind them an involucre of bracts, which after the ray florets have fallen open out in a starry manner. They are light, silvery, papery in appearance. Like many other things they need to be groomed before they can be used. Clean out the faded petals and strip the stems of dead leaves before arrangement.

These starry shapes look well cut with short stems and grouped as focal points in an arrangement of dark green ivy, black privet and rose hips. If you do this use a few taller stars at higher levels to link one zone with the other. This is a plant which leaves us a pleasant legacy we can enjoy in winter.

Forming thick mats of its dark green, finely cut leaves, the yarrow, *Achillea millefolium*, can usually be seen at the roadside growing in great quantities. It is also a garden weed, trespassing mainly on the lawns. The flowers are long lasting, their scent and that of the foliage pleasantly pungent.

There are many garden species of achillea and some varieties of the wild plant are grown. Those you see growing wild are mainly white, but occasionally rose-coloured flowers can be found. These are very beautiful, and there are some people who grow this form as a garden plant. I like to use the flat, rosy corymbs in autumn decorations with blackberries, together with the dark leaves and red stems of dogwood and any other deep crimson foliage I can find.

The plant begins to flower in June and goes on generally until August, but you can often find blooms much later than this. Once again the late blooms seem to last longest when cut. The flat umbels, which remind me of thick old lace, hold their own with heavy, full-coloured berries and leaves of all kinds, and the touch of white brought by the flowers to an arrangement is quite pleasing.

The common teasel, *Dipsacus fullonum*, has been playing a decorative role of some kind or another for many, many years. Dyed, glittered, flocked or in its natural state, it appears in many winter or perpetuelle arrangements and decorations in interiors varying from crowded Victorian to sparse contemporary. You will find it growing usually towering above a hedgerow or along a ditch or in some place where the plants can follow a line of moist soil.

Birds and insects need teasels. The first visit the seeding heads for the oily seeds, the second, apart from searching for honey, can often be found drinking from the little reservoirs of dew and rain which form in the cupped bases of the leaves. I like to grow a plant or two in the garden, not necessarily to pick but mainly because I find it such an entertaining plant in many ways. In winter it has a striking silhouette when seen against empty, grey skies.

When teasels are in flower they are very pretty, and the soft lilac blue of the purple flowers which stud the cone-shaped involucre are reminiscent of a near relation, the wild scabious. It is possible to gather the flowers at this stage and let them dry off naturally in the vase after they have served their purpose as fresh flowers, or alternatively simply remove them and hang them upside-down to dry in the usual way. But take care if you use them fresh, for if they are cut too young they may refuse to take water.

Teasel stems are branching and usually have to be divided for flower arrangement. It is possible easily to lengthen short side stems which are cut away by mounting them on long, heavy florist wire, 18-gauge. The wire should be inserted in the base of the cut stem until you can feel it become firmly embedded in the pithy centre. Alternatively stems can be spliced with adhesive tape to fine wands of willow, privet or some similar slender subjects.

Not well known, and appearing only locally and on limy or chalky soils by the waterside, is the small teasel, *D. pilosus*. This is a pretty little teasel which one would hate to see disappear. Gather it after it has dried naturally on the plant. Shake the head to release the seeds on the ground where it grew and save just a pinch to grow at home.

Most flower arrangers are fascinated by thistles, those with gardens often growing a selection ranging from the woolly leaved onopordon, the milk-spotted silybum, blue eringium to silver-grey artichokes and cardoons.

Many of the wild thistles appeal to the decorator, so much so that certain species are imported by the florist sundriesman. One of these is the spiny carline thistle, *Carlina vulgaris*, which you will find in bloom on limy soils from July to September. Much later than this you can see—and gather—the dried, spent flower heads, for they are extremely persistent. Composed of spinous green-purple outer bracts and stiff white inner ones, which look like petals or rays of a daisy, surrounding purple florets, this thistle is 'wide-eyed', and I find it useful for arranging at the centre of ensembles of mixed dried materials.

As you would expect, the colours are best if you gather fresh thistles and dry them. Take my tip and strip off the lower leaves right away. Whether you decide to leave some foliage on is up to you. I like to retain the leaves which grow just under the bloom because they give it a little more importance from the decorative point of view. This is an extremely short-stemmed flower, and so for certain arrangements the thistles will need to be mounted on false stems. It is usually a simple matter to insert a florist's wire up inside the stem as recommended for teasels.

Carline thistles blend attractively with driftwood, and you can make some pleasant permanent decorations using these components with bracken, lichen and grasses, arranging the thistles low in the design, nestled in against the wood and contrasting with it in texture and form.

From time to time I have used the hooked bracted common

burdock, *Actium pubens*. The small, thistle-like flowers, borne several to a stem and blooming in August and September, are attractive and dry well, but they have a disconcerting habit of hooking themselves to other things in an arrangement. This can happen both as you are assembling a decoration or trying to dismantle one.

On the other hand, used alone towering above some lower grouped materials such as its own leaves and rough bark, these flowering stems can look very handsome. If they are to be dried they must be gathered before they are mature, otherwise they will tend to disintegrate.

When we were children we made burdock 'flights', using long wing feathers and individual flowers. The sharpened end of the quill was pushed into the soft base of the flower from the petal end downward. One held the feather and aimed. The burdock hooked itself on the target, usually the coat or dress of someone walking ahead, an ingenious way of using nature's method of dispersal of burdock seeds to suit our own ends!

Burdock foliage is extremely handsome. If the plant appears as a weed in your garden (it is a little too persistent in some parts of mine) lift the whole root while it is young and still small enough to use entire and set it, like a great flower, at the base of some tall branch festooned with creeper—bryony, for instance.

Common everywhere, appearing even along hedgerows in towns and suburbs, is the dainty flowered *Lapsana communis*, or nipplewort. The fine, wiry stems reaching two feet, and sometimes much more, have tiny yellow, dandelion-like flowers which bloom from July to September.

I use the flowers sometimes, especially when I want some fine, frail-looking, tall-stemmed subject to taper off an arrangement for me, but I find a greater use for the seed stems, either green or dried. And I take the precaution each autumn of gathering a really good handful, which I cut as long as possible. These need no special treatment if they have already dried on the plant. Simply strip them of leaves and stand them in a container until needed.

Lapsana seed stems can be divided and used in very small decorations. They look well in pictures and other styles of montage. So far as shape and size are concerned they provide one with an easily found material which falls half way between tiny flowers and grasses.

The tall, finely branching stems are ideal for bringing height to all kinds of arrangements. One of the most pleasing ways of using them, and a simple one, is to stand them massed fairly generously in a vase holding preserved leaves, in such a way that the foliage spreads out in a zone below the lapsana.

One of the most enchanting flowers of late summer and autumn is surely the common toadflax, *Linaria vulgaris*, which begins to bloom in July and goes on until October (*see* Pl. 25).

You used to see it in drifts along miles of roadsides. I remember it particularly on the London road from Beaconsfield, but lately it has disappeared from some haunts and I pray that a more sensitive regard for the joys and the therapeutic value of roadside verges by the powers that be will result in the general return of this charming plant. So unless you are surrounded by other blooms do not gather the flowers. If there are plenty, gather them with care and enjoy their long life spent in water, for they are good lasters. I like to use just a few stems in mixtures of wild clematis blooms, berries and foliage. The pale yellow, snapdragon-like flowers with their orange lips blend harmoniously with most others in season at the same time, be they of summer or autumn.

Another yellow flower, but quite different in appearance, is the tansy, *Tancetum vulgare*. It is quite tall, some three or four feet when in bloom. You can dry the rayless flower heads successfully if you gather them as soon as they are mature. Dry them quickly if possible in an airing cupboard. I go to the tansy plant long before it blooms because I like its leaves, deep green, several inches long and deeply cut. These are so useful in all-foliage arrangements and also to arrange with flowers that have little foliage of their own (*see* Pl. 23). The leaves, like the flowers, are pungent.

In retrospect it seems to me that the sunny farm lanes and the ways through fields around Bath where I lived as a child were lined with the wild marjoram, *Origanum vulgare*. Certainly to me the plant is now synonymous with summer holidays from school. It is so easy to recall the pungently scented air the dust kicked up as we walked chattering along, insufficiently appreciating the mass of flowers around us, taking them as our natural right, regarding them as there for ever.

This plant grows profusely on calcareous soils. Once on the south coast I found a pure white variety growing, but normally the rosy-purple flowers bloom all through July and September. I am happy to say that you can find great areas of it on the Cotswolds. If you are wise you will gather a bunch and dry some sprigs for cooking. The flowers are both delightful and long lasting in an arrangement. I enjoy the contrast of soft, flowery texture against firm fruits of darker hue, blackberries and elderberries in particular.

This marjoram is well worth growing in the garden. You can buy the seeds quite easily. Although I grow mine on my herb bank I also have a root or two in a mixed border where it furnishes the soil prettily and decoratively for many months.

Some of my favourite flowers of late summer and autumn are the golden hypericums, which range from shrubby species like the androseamum and calycinum to the tremulous pulchrum, so aptly named 'beautiful St John's wort', and the tiny creeping humifusum, common on gravel soils and heaths. Fortunately the description 'common' can be applied to many of them, and judging by the way some spring up in my own garden it is really surprising that there are not more to be seen. Even so, some are seen only locally, so one should really learn to know them before picking them indiscriminately.

Growing on calcareous soils and flowering from early June until late September, sometimes even later depending on the season, is the *Hypericum perforatum*, or perforate St John's wort. Like all the others it has the beautiful central cluster of fine stamens, and is identified by its yellow petals with tiny black dots. I note that the Royal Horticultural Society's *Dictionary of Gardening* says of this plant: 'Garden weed in Britain, though quite a pretty one.' It appeared as a weed in our garden and has been allowed to stay where it was found growing, in a mixed border. I am grateful to it, not only for the summer-long blooming but also for its warm russet seed heads and stems, which I leave on all winter to bring a note of warm colour to the garden. Its flowers, like all the others, need to be well hardened before arrangement or they will not take water properly.

A very dainty little flower, its corymbs much more branched than those of perforatum, but the individual blooms smaller and the buds prettily red-tipped, is the square-stalked St John's wort, *H. tetrapterum*, which grows prolifically in bogs and at stream sides. But don't confuse this with the wavy St John's wort, *H. undulatum*, which also likes moist conditions, but is more locally confined to parts of the West Country and south Wales.

I imagine that many people who proudly display a bank of rose of Sharon, *H. calycinum*, at the front of their house or along the side of a drive, would be surprised to learn that those gorgeous, almost unbelievably beautiful, blooms are produced by one of our native plants. And how adaptable it is too! It will grow almost anywhere, even under trees where most plants pine because they lack the sunlight and cannot tolerate the heavy drips from the dense foliage overhead. How right gardeners were to bring it into cultivation, but on the other hand how could they avoid it? For it is one of the most beautiful plants in cultivation and hardy enough to grow unhampered in our demanding climate.

If you want to use rose of Sharon in arrangements, gather the flowers in bud, just before they are ready to open. The stems are shrubby, so be sure to harden them properly. Later on don't disdain the pointed green seed cases. These are extremely attractive, especially in all green and foliage arrangements.

As much as I love and admire *H. calycinum* I must confess that I find *H. androsemum* equally endearing, possibly because it offers more variety to both the gardener and the flower arranger.

It is seen growing wild, mostly in the west, preferring the moist air and coolth of damp hedgerows and ditches, a fact which I find interesting because in my garden it grows in sun and shade alike and equally well. Known as the tutsan, its leaves have a sweet smell when bruised, and for this reason the plant is also called amber or sweet amber because of the similarity of the scent to ambergris. I can't imagine our garden without this plant. A small shrub some two to three feet tall, it begins to bloom in June. The flowers, each about three-quarters of an inch across, grow in terminal clusters or cymes, nicely nestled and contrasted by large green opposite leaves. These leaves, incidentally, often have to be cut neatly away when you come to arrange the stems or else you may find that you have much foliage and little shape to the arrangement.

While some flowers are still blooming the fruits, really berry-like capsules, appear from the earlier blooms and so you have stems with yellow flowers, green, orange and then red 'berries' all in one cluster, very beautiful indeed! Later, when the capsules mature, they become first brown and then black. Their texture changes, and instead of the gleaming berry-like shine they take on a wooden appearance. They retain their shape and are firm and long lasting. I find them so useful for all kinds of perpetuelle arrangements. They should be gathered as soon as they are ripe so that they keep in good condition.

In the garden I let them stay on the plant all winter and cut the faded stems away in spring. Judging by the many seedlings which appear everywhere the fruits are much appreciated by the birds. We like them too, but for a different reason. They furnish the winter scene and soften the stark appearance peculiar to gardens that are all too eagerly tended and tidied in the autumn.

nine

Winter

It interests me that, as I write and recall plants I have known, and flowers I have gathered and arranged, it is those decorations I have made in winter that come first to my mind. Obviously it is not for the mass of brilliant flowers that I remember them, but even so none were colourless. All their subdued hues have given me pleasure, sometimes unexpected.

I remember walking with my husband and son on a Mendip hilltop in late January and finding some ivy, not green but wine-coloured, covering an area of an old limestone wall. Treasure trove indeed! The foliage was extremely beautiful and, like all ivy, very long lasting. These trails and leaves were used time and time again. And even in death they played a happy role, for when at last they refused to take water any longer I used some of them in a dried flower arrangement, while a few of the brightest leaves went into the great dried flower montage which decorates the wall above our bed.

While they were fresh and glowing these ivy trails, and the large leaves taken from low down in the stem and arranged individually, were used with a variety of materials; with matching ruby-red bare stems of dogwood, harmonizing with bare orange and tawny willow stems, they brought colour to dried seed heads and I used them with bought flowers. I recall how charming they looked with rose-coloured freesias.

We are not all lucky enough to find such unusual coloured foliage, but the ivy itself is plentiful everywhere and no one need ever be without green in winter in this country.

The shape of the leaves and the habit of growth varies in the young and adult stage of this plant, and it is not until it has reached the fullness of years that it flowers. You will find it in bloom from mid October, the creamy-green clusters produced on branching woody stems which have pointed leaves, unlike the characteristic shape of the young foliage.

These flowers last well when cut and they blend well with a great many of the shop flowers, but they have one great disadvantage in that they are extremely attractive to bluebottles and large flies. You will sometimes see the growing plants thick with them. The flies will find their way indoors somehow, simply to feast on the nectar in the flowers.

I prefer to wait for the berries, green-black in round clusters, which form in November and last on the plants right into the spring months unless the pigeons are hungry.

During winter these fruits can form the basis of many decorations. They look well as the firm, dense mass needed at the foot of line subjects such as driftwood, bare branches or catkin-draped twigs. I like to see them in bowls for table decorations, arranged low with some flower or another rising above the dark mass. My shop flower favourites with these berries are chincherinchees, red anemones and white freesias, not mixed, but one kind of flower only contrasting with the dark fruits and glossy, deep green leaves.

Many people who use these berries in Christmas decorations like to paint and embellish them in various ways, sometimes entirely dipped in white. I don't like this myself, for I find the true colour so beautiful even though it can be sombre. What I prefer to do for party decorations is to touch each of the berries lightly with a little paint and the lightest touching of frost glitter in the centre of each. This is done quickest by first painting and then upturning the berries and dipping the cluster in the glitter. The leaves too can be made to look a little more party-like if they are just margined with frost, more attractive, I think, than if they are heavily frosted over the entire leaf surface.

You can use ivy trail as a framework for other flowers. This will last several weeks, even several months sometimes. However, for this to be really successful you should choose the trails carefully.

Those torn off tree trunks or prised from walls are often too brittle to be attractively or easily arranged. It is much better to look for trails which have not rooted into anything. You can usually find these topping a wall or running over a bank.

If you find that some of the ivy trails root in water, and they often do, you have the beginnings of an ivy plant which can either continue to grow indoors or which can be planted in the garden or in a window box.

Sometimes the ivy you gather will have made roots and you need not cut these off, for rooted ivy will go on growing in water, moss, Florapak, Oasis or sand. In fact you could make a little pebble-and-water arrangement of rooted ivy trails and decorate these from time to time by arranging little flowers among them.

Quite often near a living plant you can find one that has died, or perhaps instead there are some dead stems on the main plant. At other times you will find dead ivy hanging from a tree trunk because the main stem has been severed at ground level. Sometimes the dead wood has become peeled, bleached and polished by wind, sun and rain so that it looks like driftwood. This is well worth collecting. Ivy root wood, that which grows flat against trees, is highly prized by some decorators, so much so that it is on sale in shops which specialize in florists' sundries. This is bare, not unlike driftwood, but sometimes this effect has been gained by scraping the bark and adventitious roots away, and the root wood shows strong markings as a consequence.

Personally I don't find this type of accessory attractive, for it shows only too clearly its eagerness and artificiality. With a little patience and labour you can peel the bark off in a much more natural manner. Let the root wood soak for a time in rainwater. Test it from time to time to see if the water has become slimy. This is unpleasant, I know, but it is the only effective way to make sure that the bark will peel easily. By the time the water is foul you will find that the bark can be pulled away and you will see the smooth surface of the wood below. When it dries it will be lighter in colour.

Where you find the wild clematis growing in the south, there you can expect to find box, *Buxus sempervirens*. It too flourishes on calcareous soils, from Gloucestershire to Kent, although you may not find it growing so plentifully as the creeper. There are localities, however, where it grows very freely indeed, the ancient trees, broad and handsome, appearing to sit on the chalky hillsides.

Like most evergreens box is long lasting, especially in winter when the foliage is well matured. It has a bunchy and branching habit and one good stem can often be divided to provide several flat sprays to contrast with flowers of rounded outline in many arrangements. The glossy green of the leaves looks well contrasted with white flowers. I like to use chincherinchees, early narcissi and snowdrops with box. There is also drama when box is used with the vivid colours such as you see in anemones, daffodils, early tulips, carnations and freesias. Possibly because it is such a deep, rich green and because it gleams, it also looks well with fruits and berries, not necessarily wild ones only. Bright red peppers, tangerines, apples and green box can make an attractive party decoration.

I like to use masses of short snippets of box for many kinds of Christmas decorations. Some of these are described in Chapter Ten.

Box can be preserved in glycerine and water, when it will turn a deep leathery brown. Sprays of this look marvellous with brown cones and seed heads of all kinds, especially if you have some of the arching, graceful sprays of larch cones to use with them. Brown metal vases, popular as clock sets in Victorian times, dark wooden containers, including modern designs as well as old polished canisters, admirably suit treated leaves which look brown and polished after preservation. If you make an arrangement of mixed perpetuelles the box will prove invaluable because of the dainty tapering appearance of the slender, trimmed sprays of neat oval leaves.

Like the box the native yew, *Taxus baccata*, favours limy and chalky soils, so where you find one you are likely to find the other. In spring in March and April the dense dark green shoots become smothered with tiny yellow flowers, and for a while the yew is reminiscent of mimosa, but in winter the sprays should be used with discretion or they will dominate all else in an arrangement. Their greatest value lies in the habit of growth, for those flat-backed branches can form the basic elements of many Christmas decorations, from table centres to welcome swags for the front door. I have more to say about this plant in the following chapter.

Not unexpectedly the plants most associated with traditional Christmas decorations, the ivy, yew, box and holly, are all native plants. The holly, *Ilex aquifolium*, is surely one of the loveliest of all our trees when it is in fruit, but before you help yourself remember that the farmer should surely have first cut of the crop. After all, it grows on his land, and although the trees are common in woods and hedges and may seem free for all, remember that they are often left to grow so that they may be cut to help make a little extra profit. Often to help oneself is to steal.

Once the legal aspect is determined, permission sought and received, no one should go gathering holly without secateurs. A torn and mutilated tree, such as is so often cruelly seen on the roadsides in the country, will die long before its time. Gather the holly carefully and with an eye to both the shape and the well-being of the plant. Don't be tempted to take more than you really need.

The berries grow close to the stem, often hidden or partially concealed by the leaves. I like always to snip away some of the foliage so that I can get greater colour value from the berries. Usually it is those on the lower part of the stem that are best removed, but this is something which must be determined by the style of the arrangement and the part the holly is to play. When berried holly is really plentiful I sometimes trim off all the leaves so that I can use the berried sprigs as glowing focal points among holly leaves and other evergreens.

Don't hesitate to use any other kind of red berry with holly if it has no fruit of its own. Clusters of rose hips and haws and berries from garden shrubs such as pyracantha and cotoneaster look very attractive, and some years when the holly berry crop is small they are essential.

Often in woods and along roadsides the blind or berry-less holly is abundant. Don't disdain it. Even plain green holly sprigs are both useful and decorative in festival arrangements (*see* Pls. 34–35). They look well with bought flowers. Bright anemones will bring the complementary red of the berries to the glossy leaves. White and yellow spray type chrysanthemums, especially those starry anemone-centred varieties, will gain beauty and a touch of holiday magic from the dark green of the holly. Smooth imported gladioli can be made to tower above a knot of the spiny foliage.

When you gather sprigs avoid if you can the stiff, straight stems with leaves set close together and select instead the thinner, more pliant growths which will curve delightfully when arranged. And before you arrange the holly, or indeed any evergreen, wash it. For holly I use a soft brush and clean tepid water, and it is surprising just how much dirt is loosened from leaves and stem. The holly gleams and is much greener after treatment.

If you do not wish to buy flowers you will find that rose hips, the seed pods of *Iris foetidissima*, bryony and snowberries if massed generously enough make gorgeous arrangements. It isn't only the growing leaves that are useful. Search the ground below the tree (wear gloves) and among the fallen leaves you will find many that have become naturally skeletonized or nearly so. These, after some grooming and preparation, will make delightful Christmas decorations that can often be kept from year to year. There is more about them in my final chapter.

Although all through late summer and autumn they are there, green and slowly darkening, shaped like doll's house bunches of grapes, it is in winter that privet berries become really conspicuous. Then they are glossy black, and they grow thick and branching on their long, pliant stems.

Privet berries at all stages of maturity can be used in all kinds of flower arrangements, but invariably you will find that the stems must be pruned if they are to look their best and if they are to be arranged easily. Otherwise the many snags and the lateral bunches of berries tend to catch in the other materials and impede assembly.

The short side stems are useful in low arrangements. I like to use them as a main fabric in low bowls. Short-stemmed pieces make cones and globes for party decorations. The slender branches are pliable and can often be easily bowed or curved to follow the line and patterns required of them by the design into which they are to be set. I think that it is well worth while grading them, for some of the bunches are dense and heavy while others have no more than a few berries to them.

These berries, though black, when fresh glow attractively, each tiny fruit with a little point of light reflected back. I like to arrange them with other wild materials of course, but they also look splendid with all kinds of black-centred bought and garden flowers such as anemones of all colours and early tulips. And, like grapes, privet berries look well with all kinds of flowers simple or choice, so don't hesitate to use them with such blooms as roses, carnations and small chrysanthemums. On the other hand they are handsome enough to stand on their own. I was once lucky enough to find a vase shaped like a great mussel shell standing on one end. In this I arranged privet berries with imported bleached adiantum fern, and I finished the design with the title Black Pearls. It gave a great deal of pleasure.

The tall Scots pine, *Pinus sylvestris*, has tufted, graceful branches that can be used in many attractive ways. I find them particularly evocative when used in the picture story type of arrangement. For the classic line of ancient Japanese arrangements, for Ikebana and other oriental styled decorations, this pine tree offers interesting and easily arranged materials (*see* Pl. 6).

A branch or two on a heavy pinholder in a low dish is a delightful foil for one, two or more choice flowers at any time of the year, but the style is especially useful in winter. The tree's trunk becomes barer as it becomes taller, and one cannot always gather branches easily, almost invariably there are a few branches to be found lying on the ground under a tree, and this is particularly the case after a storm.

The student will find it helpful to study the manner in which the branches grow on the tree. From the ground one almost always sees them hanging prettily pendent. It is well worth trying to recapture the same line in an arrangement at home, for it is a most effective style in which to display this pine.

I find that tall slim containers are useful here, especially those with clear-cut modern lines, for these stand high enough to allow you to let the pine go free and to assume the attractive angle in which the pine needles seem to be reaching out to the sun and air (*see* Pl. 29).

The ancient Japanese flower teachers had a rule about pine. When branches were used, the rule stated, the needles should flow or fall always away from the centre of the stem, never over it to hide it. Japanese rules were usually based on sensitive observance of a plant or some law of nature, and fortunately by following them one also panders to aesthetic pleasure. So if when you go to gather some of this pine you take notice of how the needles hang in relation to the way the branch grows you should understand why this rule was insisted upon. If when the pine is arranged in a vase you are able to capture the same direction of the flow of the needles that you saw on the plant when it was growing you are sure to be pleased with your placement of the branches.

The ground under Scots pines is often thick with cones. If you would like to know more about using these, see the following chapter.

Picea abies, formerly *P. excelsa*, the common spruce, Norway or

Norwegian spruce, or spruce fir, is the Christmas tree, one of the best known of all forest trees. You are not likely to find it growing naturally, for it is widely planted, yet it is such a feature of our countryside, more so perhaps than many other conifers which are used in forestry, that I feel I should include it in this book. Fortunately it is possible to buy bundles of the cut branches, so I shall limit my remarks on the decorative values of this plant to the way in which it can be used at Christmas time. You will find them in the next chapter.

One of the commonest trees in the countryside and one of the most distinctive, yet not native, is the larch, *Larix decidua*. You will see it also planted in great numbers by the Forestry Commission, in whose plantations it changes like the sky according to season, sometimes a light tan which becomes smudged with spring green, growing ever stronger until in summer it is as dark as pines, yet in autumn it turns colour again, growing every day a little more golden, for the larch is deciduous, a rarity among conifers.

This graceful tree serves flower arrangers well in all its seasons. I find it particularly beautiful both in leaf and bare. The graceful, tenuous stems afford infinite pleasure even though they are sometimes a little difficult to arrange. The mature cones are as lovely as little wooden roses and can be used in a hundred ways. When young and immature they are the brightest ruby-red and beautiful beyond words, and in summer when they are larger they are jade green. From autumn onwards they grow a deeper and deeper brown.

Spent branches are jettisoned the year round, and even the most casual inspection of the ground under a tree is rewarding. The cones are not loose and scattered over the ground as they are under the Scots pine, but instead are still attached to their branches, and often so beautifully spaced and arranged that they are ready prepared for arrangement. I could write a chapter on larch alone.

For winter arrangements the slender curving branches can be used to accentuate the lines of an arrangement, especially when short-stemmed blooms such as Christmas roses are used. One of my prettiest December decorations was made with larch, variegated holly, daffodils and gold tree baubles all arranged on a pinholder in a brass bowl.

Permanent decorations made of preserved leaves, 'wooden'

accessories such as cones, nuts and seed pods are often improved by the inclusion of the tapering larch stems, and if you treat the cones as flowers, cutting long stems into sections so that each stem bears one or more cones, you will find that you have delightful items to arrange and mass at rim level and elsewhere.

For Christmas I like to use a goblet and make a pyramidal outline of larch stems, in front of which I mass holly, ivy and wild clematis and then finally a centre knot of larch cones and berries. I use larch cones in many forms of both Christmas and permanent decorations such as mirror swags, and there are more details in the following pages.

Those who have watched the progress of flower arrangement will know that the humble yet often showy broom, *Sarothamnus scoparius*, often plays an important, and a surprisingly sophisticated, role in modern designs. It is as important when it is bare and virtually leafless as it is when gay with bright yellow pea-like blooms.

Its graceful green branches, often shaped artificially by the arranger (for gentle pressure will induce curves that will remain as required), can provide the upwards sweep, the final flourish or the full Hogarth curve of a variety of modern and line arrangements. These curving, graceful lines suit particularly well the many leafless flowers which are on sale in winter and early spring. A curve of yellow daffodils, for instance, arranged to follow the same lines of a crescent made by the curving broom stems, all resting on a round dish, will make a pleasing harmony of curves and spring colour.

In tall, cylindrical vases broom can be arranged to make one tall sweeping curve, the top of an S, to occupy the higher zones of the arrangement, while the lower part of the S, beginning at rim level to reach down at least half way the depth of the container, is made by moving the stems at an angle to the portion pushed inside the container, nothing like so difficult as it sounds. Flowers or other plant materials can then be arranged within the curving limits of this 'lazy S' or Hogarth curve. By using swathes of broom this way a few blooms only can be employed to great advantage. And if you want to retain this background you can, for broom will dry quite easily. If you care to pick it green, and then tie it in the required curves and store it, you will have some useful floradashery to draw upon from time to time. You can use these dried pieces in fresh or perpetuelle arrangements. Often the stems have to be pruned and thinned before arrangement so as to avoid density and also to accentuate gradation to a fine tip.

Although it is only natural in winter that our thoughts should turn first to those plants which remain green, there are others which are not evergreen but which are sufficiently decorative in their own right to be included in many schemes. There are some which have brightly coloured barks, the dogwood *Cornus* or *Thelycrania sanguinea*, for example. This has warm, crimson-red twigs. The willows vary considerably according to their species, some being a burnt orange, others yellow, some purple.

They all look well either mixed or on their own seen against the neutrality of a white or some other lightly tinted wall. Contrasted this way one can enjoy the silhouette of the stems as well as the subtle warm tones and the smooth texture of the barks.

Quite often, after a while indoors, these stems will begin to shoot and their soft, silky leaves will begin to emerge and expand. In time even the round heads of immature blossom buds of the dogwood are revealed. These seldom if ever open completely in water, but even so the tiny immature corymbs are very appealing and carry in their clusters a promise of spring soon to come.

From midwinter you can expect to see catkins of all kinds more in evidence, their conspicuity depending upon the mildness or otherwise of the season. As I said in the chapter on spring, you can begin to pick pussy willow as soon as the branches are smudged with the grey silk.

Hazel and alder catkins probably open indoors more quickly than any of the other trees or shrubs. You can ensure a continual show of these merely by picking a branch or two each week. One should never pick catkins once they are fully open and already spilling their pollen, for they will not then last long in water and will even fall soon after they are gathered. Hazel branches often grow flat, especially on young wood. Curved and more interestingly shaped branches are found on old trees. Even then the branch is likely to need pruning and shaping for arrangement.

The curly, dark branches of alder are particularly attractive and are valuable in giving an evocative line to an arrangement. The pendulous, cone-like structures of the previous summer remain on the tree all winter, so that they and the young catkins may be found on the branch together at the same time. This makes them doubly useful because the branches are so well furnished that they need little else with them.

I like to use them, tall, well silhouetted, in both low and tall containers and to arrange a knot of flowers and/or leaves at their foot or at rim level. Often I ignore the colour value of the alder, which is fairly neutral anyway, and concentrate on matching the container with the other materials. One of the arrangements I most remember was in a striped mug, blue-green and brown on white, and I used dried hydrangea heads and leathery brown camellia leaves.

Almost all twigs and branches will open in the warmth of a room, and sometimes a simple pitcher of a mixed bunch is as pleasing an arrangement as any other style. I always look for the *Viburnum lantana* as soon as the days begin to draw out a little. The mealy clusters of immature buds tip long, straight branches. I find these particularly attractive, and I have used them for years with all kinds of shop flowers. I like them with daffodils and the forced Dutch iris. They are extremely long lasting and fairly static in growth.

The sturdy, smooth stems of the horse chestnut, topped with the deep brown pointed buds, known affectionately to most of us as 'sticky buds', must surely be among the most favoured of all winter decorations. Quite often all we see are a few stems standing alone in a vessel, yet these are ideal companions for other plant materials. A few stems carefully placed will bring height and importance of line to the smallest number of winter flowers such as narcissi or tulips (*see* Pl. 11).

The longevity of the buds, which open gradually in water revealing soft downy leaves like baby hands reaching for the light, is a great advantage, for it means that a framework made from them will go on for weeks, lending support and body to the few fleeting flowers which have to be replaced more frequently.

If you study a horse chestnut tree as it grows you will notice that every stem tip turns upwards with an attractive flourish, each reaching to the sun. Yet when we arrange sticky buds we almost always tend to place them vertically. The habit of growth on the tree demonstrates how much more dramatic the branches would look if they were sometimes arranged to flow either downwards or horizontally.

Surely this indicates that these are good stems for Ikebana and other stylized forms of arrangement. There is more about this plant in Chapter Six, on spring, but the habit of growth under discussion leads me to a few observations on winter arrangement generally.

Once the leaves have fallen from the trees we have a wonderful opportunity to admire and study their silhouettes, and there is much we can learn about flower arrangement from them, as I suggested in the chapter on Arrangement (Chapter Three). Meanwhile the gnarled, smooth, lichened, contorted, curved, upright or pendent branches all around us are a reminder that this is the season for creating and featuring lovely outlines and scenes from the branches themselves.

You can have an engaging time by trying to reproduce the pattern of a tree, not necessarily with its own branches, although naturally there is pleasure to be gained in this, but with all kinds of stems, even flowers. Try making a poplar shape with broom branches and following an elm's outline with seed pods.

Where a lone branch is arranged, as I have suggested, in a low dish, fixed firmly on a pinholder, its base can be decorated in many ways yet with really few materials. You can use mossy stones, small plants, moss tufts, wood bark, fern fronds, skeleton leaves, sprays of ivy, late berries and many other materials in a series of evocative picture story arrangements.

In the early days of January and on into March, and in mild winters in particular, many weeds with tiny flowers are in bloom —chickweed, speedwell, groundsel and even daisies—according to the part of the country one lives in. None of these little blooms could be said to be distinctive, but unity is strength even where colour is concerned. If they can be gathered and each species made into a tight little posy they can be treated as one short-stemmed large bloom. They will play many a pretty role grouped together at the foot of a curving branch of early blossom, opening sticky buds or even sun-dried driftwood. Bunched tiny flowers have better colour value than when used singly, although these are delightful in miniatures (*see* Pls. 7–10).

In the same way that the winter skeletons of the trees are beautiful, exciting and instructive, so are the bare stems of many of the seed heads one finds, bereft, along the waysides and in hedgerows or on the margins of woods and watersides. The umbelliferae especially have great beauty, and if you gather them try arranging them so that they are seen against the light, where you will be able to appreciate the structure of the umbels to the full.

Don't hesitate to mix the old with the new. There is really no point in dividing them into strict zones. In the countryside the fresh new grass will be pushing up through the fawn, faded blades of last year, and the young shoots in the hedgerows will soon be showing through the fluted stems of the hogweed and thrusting the graceful though faded brome grass aside. You can mix them in the same way and enjoy them almost as much at home.

ten

Festival Time

'Who goes a-mothering gathers violets in the lane', used to be so applicable to my friends and me when we were children. Most of us knew where the earliest blooms were to be found on the warmest face of banks and hedgerows, and the keenest of us were out soonest on Mothering Sunday to search for our gift posies. And violets they had to be.

For some reason it was considered 'one up' upon one's friends to be the first to find white violets, and up higher still if you found also the red form, really a dusky wine hue. Sometimes an early primrose or two would be included in the posy, another bit of one-upmanship, but the pretty ground ivy, though as blue in hue as the violet and so often misleading accordingly, was rejected. If violets were few the posy was made larger by a thicker than usual collar of leaves, ivy if there were not sufficient of the flower's own foliage. What they lacked in numbers, though, the flowers always made up for in perfume.

These flowers are still to be found, though not in such numbers, and anyway lanes are not now places to dawdle searching for shy blooms. A great part of the significance of our little gifts was surely that we had gathered them ourselves. I am sure that they were much more appreciated by our mothers than a bought bunch would have been, unless of course there was evidence that certain effort had gone into amassing the sum needed to buy it.

I am old-fashioned enough to think that there is something special about a home-produced Mothering Sunday gift, and there are so many kinds of delightful arrangements which can be made from simple wild things, incorporating green moss, leaves and trails, the first new shoots, catkins and blossoms from many shrubs and trees, coltsfoot, winter heliotrope, violets, celandines and other little flowers in season. Offerings made from any of these need cost no more than the odd penny or two, if that.

Empty waterproof cartons of many shapes and sizes can be found near at hand, including almost all the plastic, expendable types such as yoghurt cartons, meat dishes, egg cases, even cheese holders. If necessary these can be lined with foil or strong plastic to make them waterproof. They can also be covered with foil to hide the descriptions on the containers where printing exists. By the time they have been filled in such a way that trails, fronds and leaves or little sprigs hang over the rim, their mundane quality and their original purpose will be disguised.

Low containers such as meat packs can be filled with attractive green moss, the finest fronds pulled up from the mass a little so that they resemble fern fronds, and the bed of moss itself, studded with whatever flowers, clusters of blossom and young leaves can be found. So much depends both upon the season and the date of Mothering Sunday. This is not a constant date, but varies according to the Church calendar and it is always the fourth Sunday in Lent.

Shells of all kinds make attractive containers for Mothering Sunday gifts. Children might enjoy making a miniature arrangement in a large, empty snail shell if no other kinds are available. These can usually be found, whitened by age and weather, in a bank or at the foot of a hedge. Most shells, including the snail, will need a base so that they will stand upright. An upturned bottle top suits a snail and gives it an easy-to-hold foot, but the shells also look pretty fixed to a small piece of bark. Any strong adhesive will fix one to the other.

Easter gift arrangements can be made on much the same lines. Eggshells will hold water and small flowers quite effectively. If these are not held in eggcups these too will need bases. The eggcups themselves make attractive vases, the old-fashioned ones being little pedestal vases.

An old bird's nest found in a hedge can be foil-lined and filled with flowers. Little baskets always seem in character for this type of gift, and these can be both easily and prettily filled with tiny posies of flowers and blossom resting on a bed of moss.

Gipsies used to sell primrose roots held in simple baskets which they made from willow. These are quite easy for a child to make and they can be used very effectively for all kinds of flower arrangements. They are made of eight equal lengths of willow, each three to four inches long, depending on the size of the basket to be made, and one longer piece for the handle, about twelve inches long, for the handle should stand high. The willow pieces can either be tacked or lashed together. Begin by making one square for the base by laying two lengths parallel and placing two more on them at right angles. Fix these together. Make another square following the lines of the first and fix the two squares together (*see* Pl. 32). Add the handle by fixing it to opposite sides after curving it. Line the basket to make it waterproof. Use damp moss, moist sand, water and wire-netting or well-soaked Oasis or Florapak to keep the flowers fresh and hold them in place.

This type of basket is also useful throughout the year for many kinds of flower gifts. You can also use it for Christmas decorations, when it looks attractive filled with sprigs of evergreen flowing over the edge all round and with clusters of berries and cones at the centre.

Cones can often play the role of flowers as I have already suggested, and since they are so plentiful, and no one objects to their being gathered up and taken away, decorators would be wise to lay in a good stock. They last for years so long as they are new and in good condition when they are first gathered. If they are wet they soon dry indoors.

In most cases they will need to be mounted on false stems, and quite the easiest way to do this is to use florist wires. The weight or gauge of the wire to be used will depend upon the size of the cones. Generally speaking a 20-gauge wire will be most useful for many sizes of cones, especially those of the Scots pine, and if you should be lucky enough to have any very much larger kinds you can thicken and strengthen the mount by using two or more wires together. Lighter wires are needed for smaller cones, 22- or 24-gauge or even finer for small larch and alder. The first two sizes come in 7-, 10- and 14-inch lengths, the latter being the most useful because it can always be shortened, but the finer wires are normally in 7-inch lengths only.

If the cone has a tiny stem butt at its base you may be able to fix the wire to it, but even this operation is not really easy. It is almost always better to mount the cone by easing the wire in between the scales as near to the base of the cone as possible. You need to pull on the wire quite firmly to get it down out of sight. If you leave roughly equal portions of wire on each side of the cone as you encircle it these can be brought down together as a false stem. If a little real stem exists the two ends can be twisted around it and then brought down to continue its line or, failing this, the ends should merely be twisted around each other once or twice before they are straightened. A little practice at this will soon bring skill. I like to get a quantity of cones mounted early in winter so that they are always ready.

For Christmas decorations you can group them together in many ways. For instance, you can make a door, wall, chimney or mirror swag by using a flat branch of yew or spruce as a background or base. The cones can be massed along the centre with one cone, the smallest, at the tapering base graduating to a cluster at the top. Here you can decorate the swag further by using berry clusters, ribbon bows, sprays of holly or contrasting evergreens, preserved leaves, dried umbels of hogweed, even tree baubles (*see* Pl. 36).

This is a good basic pattern which can be adapted to suit your own tastes and circumstances. Make the swag of cones first and lay them on the evergreen later. As you assemble the swag arrange the cones on the table before you so that it takes their weight. Have all the cones ready mounted on wires, and to join them simply twist the wire of the cone to be arranged around the straightened wires of those that were laid before. Begin with one cone, the end of the cone section, lay the next quite near it, twist the second wire tightly around the first at a convenient point, straighten the wires to form a spine and arrange the next one in the same way. You can face the cones in the right direction as the assembly proceeds. When you lay the finished cone section on the evergreen branch, tie one to the other at three or four places so that the two become one.

Cones mounted on shorter or shortened wires can be arranged in a Byzantine cone. For this you need a conical foundation. It is possible to buy these, made of a firm foamed plastic, but you can also make the cone of small mesh wire-netting packed tightly with damp moss. This foundation can be stood on a simple base such as a cake board, or alternatively in a goblet-shaped vase or some other footed container. If you want it to serve as a small Christmas tree it can be stood in a flowerpot. In each case the container needs to be weighted with sand or shingle. When the cone is to be arranged in a container you will find it helpful first to fix a stout cane in the centre to serve as a spine and support the cone.

Having fixed the foundation firmly in position first cover the surface with short snippets of box, yew or spruce, making the surface as even and smooth as possible. These snippets should be shorter than the cones and their ends should be cut on a slant for easy penetration of the mounting material. Begin at the base and insert the slanted ends at an angle upwards in the lower cones so that the tips flow slightly downwards. Do the opposite in the upper zones, and in the centre keep the tips horizontal. Arrange the pine cones in the same manner. The evergreens should fill in the spaces between the cones.

This again is a useful pattern and you can vary it as much as you wish, making the cone itself taller or wider as well as varying the contents. Berry clusters alternated with the cones look attractive and bring additional colour. Skeleton holly leaves, also wire-mounted, can be arranged between the cones or perhaps as a collar at the base of the cone. You can make the design entirely of cones, using very small types to fill in the spaces between the larger ones. Tufts of wild clematis look well as a filler instead of evergreens. These are just a few examples, and many more will come readily to mind when faced with available materials.

A table centre which can be decorated with cones is easily made by taking two matching branch end pieces of spruce or yew. These should lie flat, and when placed end to end the base of the stem portions, parallel for three or four inches, should measure the length of the finished decoration. Lash the stems together, making sure that the branches still lie flat. Over the tied portion tie a roll of wire-netting to hold one or more candles and any of the other components such as holly sprigs, evergreen snippets, berried stems and the cones. If you wish or if this seems advisable fix a small mat under the base as well.

If candles are used fix these in position down through the netting first. It should hold them quite firmly, but if they wobble a little hold them upright as you arrange the other stems and you will find that these wedge the candles in place and they will soon stay firm. Arrange the evergreen in the netting just as though it were in a container, letting the longest side trails follow the line of the two foundation pieces, their tips not quite reaching to the ends of these. Succeeding stems should each be a little shorter.

Decorate the centre with a group of cones glittered lightly if you wish, with berry clusters, individual ivy leaves, skeleton holly and dainty umbels both also lightly glittered.

Cones are easily glittered, and most other materials are treated in much the same way. Mount them first and then, holding them in a bunch, lightly touch the tips of the scales with colourless varnish, or you can use an aerosol spray for this. Have ready a little glitter in a paper bag and insert the cones, upside-down, in this. Gather the mouth of the bag tightly around the wire bunch and shake the bag so that the glitter inside is well distributed all over the cones. Open the bag and draw the cones out carefully, shaking them gently as you do this to remove the surplus glitter.

As well as larger cones I like to collect beech mast, acorns and any other tree seed-cases and keys I can find. Mounting them on fine wires is a little tedious, but it is worth while preparing a quantity of either single items or clusters. You can make pretty gift decorations from these, fashioning them into little posies surrounded by collars of green ivy leaves, skeleton or brown holly as well as the fresh green leaves.

These same posies can be used to make the Byzantine cone I described earlier. Several can be bound onto a hoop of willow twigs covered with evergreen to make a garland. You can make ropes of them to use as festoons for the aprons of buffet tables, to decorate the centre of a long slender branch for a wall decoration, to wreathe down around outsize candles or to make little wreaths for their bases for a party table.

I like to make a large cone or tree of strong, firm, lightly tinted paper fixed to a cakeboard and to decorate this from tip to base with a helter-skelter ornament which is in fact a long rope made of all the tiny seed cases I have described, backed with evergreen and intermingled with wild clematis seeds.

It is an unusual decoration which never fails to please and to arouse interest, and yet it costs so very little and is made mainly from windfalls which normally would be overlooked.

index

121